D0794263

Volumes in the
New Century Exceptional Lives series . . .

A Desert Daughter's Odyssey:
For All Those Whose Lives
Have Been Touched by Cancer—
Personally, Professionally
Or Through a Loved One

Sharon Wanslee

The Man Who Was Dr. Seuss:
The Life and Work of Theodor Geisel

Thomas Fensch

New Century Books

The Man Who Was Dr. Seuss

The Man Who Was Dr. Seuss

The Life and Work of Theodor Geisel

Thomas Fensch

New Century Books
P.O. Box 7113
The Woodlands, Tx., 77387-7113.

This book was printed in the United States of America.

Library of Congress Number:
00191961
ISBN: Hardcover
0-930751-11-6
ISBN: Paperback
0-930751-12-4

Contents

For . . .

Alice in truth . . .

"Behold, I make all things new . . . ."
Revelations 21:5

Acknowledgments

The author is grateful to the following sources for permission to reprint copyrighted material:
Photographs of Theodor Geisel printed with permission of Dr. Seuss Enterprises. All rights reserved.
And to Think that I Saw It on Mulberry Street
© Dr. Seuss Enterprises, L.P. 1937. All rights reserved.
The 500 Hats of Bartholomew Cubbins
© Dr. Seuss Enterprises, L.P. 1938. All rights reserved.
The Seven Lady Godivas
© Dr. Seuss Enterprises, L.P. 1939. All rights reserved.
The King's Stilts
© Dr. Seuss Enterprises, L.P. 1939. All rights reserved.
Horton Hatches the Egg
™ & © Dr. Seuss Enterprises, L.P. 1940. All rights reserved.
McElligot's Pool
© Dr. Seuss Enterprises, L.P. 1947. All rights reserved.
Thidwick, the Big-Hearted Moose
© Dr. Seuss Enterprises, L.P. 1948. All rights reserved.
Bartholomew and the Oobleck
© Dr. Seuss Enterprises, L.P. 1949. All rights reserved.
If I Ran the Zoo
© Dr. Seuss Enterprises, L.P. 1950. All rights reserved.
Scrambled Eggs Super!
© Dr. Seuss Enterprises, L.P. 1953. All rights reserved.

Key Dates in the Life of Theodor Geisel

1904 Theodor Seuss Geisel is born in Springfield, Mass., March 2, the son of Theodor Robert and Henrietta Seuss Geisel.

1921 Theodor Geisel attends Dartmouth College, where he begins writing and drawing for the *Jack-O-Lantern*, the campus magazine.

1925 Theodor Geisel graduates from Dartmouth in June.

1926–1927 Geisel attends Oxford University, in England, meets Helen Palmer and tours England and Europe.

1927 Geisel sells a cartoon to *The Saturday Evening Post*. When it is published, it bears the name "Seuss." Geisel marries Helen Palmer.

1928 Geisel begins drawing an advertising campaign under the title, "Quick Henry, The Flit." That phrase becomes nationally popular. The Flit campaign sustains him financially for 17 years.

1931 Geisel illustrates his first book, *Boners*, published by the Viking Press. His second book, *More Boners*, is published the same year.

1937 *And to Think That I Saw it on Mulberry Street* is published by The Vanguard Press, after numerous (27) rejections. It is the first Dr. Seuss book.

1938 *The 500 Hats of Bartholomew Cubbins* is published by The Vanguard Press.

1939 *The Seven Lady Godivas* is published by Random House. It is his only adult book and his only failure. It begins his life-long association with Random House and publisher Bennett Cerf. *The King's Stilts* is also published.

1940 *Horton Hatches the Egg* is published.

1940–1942 Geisel works as an editorial cartoonist for the newspaper *PM*.

1943–1946 Geisel serves in the Army U.S. Signal Corps, Information and Educational Division, under director Frank Capra; Geisel receives the Legion of Merit for his work on informational films and receives the first of three Academy Awards for his film *Hitler Lives*. (Originally written for the Army under the title *Your Job in Germany*.)

1947 *McElligot's Pool* is published. It is named a Caldecott Honor Book in children's literature. Geisel wins second Academy Award for *Design for Death* (written with Helen Geisel).

1948 *Thidwick the Big-Hearted Moose* is published by Random House. Geisel purchases a hill-top home in La Jolla, California where he will live the rest of his life.

1949 *Bartholomew and the Oobleck* is published; it too is named a Caldecott Honor Book.

1950 *If I Ran the Zoo* is published. It too, is named a Caldecott Honor Book.

1951 Geisel wins third Academy Award for the cartoon film *Gerald McBoing-Boing.*

1952 Geisel writes the script and songs and designs the sets for the film, *The 5,000 Fingers of Dr. T.* It is not successful. Geisel abandons Hollywood.

1953 *Scrambled Eggs Super!* is published.

1954 *Horton Hears a Who!* is published.

1955 *On Beyond Zebra!* is published.

1956 *If I Ran the Circus* is published. Geisel receives an honorary doctoral degree from Dartmouth College, his alma mater.

1957 *How the Grinch Stole Christmas!* is published and becomes one of his most popular books. *The Cat in the Hat* is published, the first of the Random House Beginner Books, for young readers.

1958 *The Cat in the Hat Comes Back* and *Yertle the Turtle and Other Stories* are published; Geisel becomes president of Beginner Books, a division of Random House.

1959 *Happy Birthday to You!* is published.

1960 *Green Eggs and Ham* is published, which has become—in terms of sales—Geisel's most popular book. *One Fish Two Fish Red Fish Blue Fish* is also published.

1961 *The Sneeches and Other Stories* is published. Geisel also publishes *Ten Apples Up On Top!* under the pseudonym Theo. LeSieg (Geisel spelled backwards).

1962 *Dr. Seuss's Sleep Book* is published.

1963 *Hop on Pop* and *Dr. Seuss's ABC* are published.

1965 *Fox in Sox, I Had Trouble Getting to Solla Sollew* and *I Wish I Had Duck Feet* (Theo. LeSieg, pseudonym) are all published.

1966 *Come Over to My House* (Theo LeSieg, pseudonym) is published.

1967 *The Cat in the Hat Song Book* is published.
Helen Palmer Geisel dies by her own hand October 23.

1968 *The Foot Book* is published, the first of the Bright and Early Books for readers pre: Beginner books. *The Eye Book* (Theo. LeSieg, pseudonym) is also published in the same series. Geisel receives an honorary doctoral degree from American International College. *Dr. Seuss's Lost World Revisited: A Forward Backward Glance* is published, despite a legal fight. Geisel marries Audrey Stone Diamond August 5.

1969 *I can Lick 50 Tigers Today! and Other Stories* and *My Book about Me—By Me, Myself, I Wrote It! I Drew It!* are published.

1970 *I Can Draw It Myself* and *Mr. Brown Can Moo! Can You?* are published.

1971 *I Can Write—by Me, Myself* (Theo. LeSieg, pseudonym) and *The Lorax*, about the loss of the environment are published. *The Lorax* becomes the most controversial Dr. Seuss book. He receives a Peabody Award for his television specials *How the Grinch Stole Christmas!* and *Horton Hears a Who!*

1972 *In a People House* (Theo. LeSieg, pseudonym) and *Marvin K. Mooney, Will You Please Go Now!* are published.

1973 *The Many Mice of Mr. Brice* (Theo. LeSieg, pseudonym), *Did I Ever Tell You How Lucky You Are?* and *The Shape of Me and Other Stuff* are all published.

1975 *Because a Little Bug Went Ka-Choo!* (Rosetta Stone, pseudonym), *Oh, The Thinks You Can Think!* and *Would You Rather be a Bullfrog?* (Theo. LeSieg) are published.

1976 *Hooper Humperdink. . . ? Not Him!* (Theo. LeSieg) and *The Cat's Quizzer* are published.

1977 *Try to Remember the First of Octember* (Theo. LeSieg) is published. Geisel receives an honorary doctoral degree from Lake Forest College and receives an Emmy Award for *Halloween is Grinch Night.*

1978 *I Can Read with My Eyes Shut!* is published.

1979 *Oh Say Can You Say?* is published.

1980 *Maybe You Should Fly a Jet! Maybe You Should Be a Vet!* (Theo. LeSieg) is published. Geisel receives an honorary doctoral degree from Whittier College and receives the Laura Ingalls Wilder Award from the American Library Association.

1981 *The Tooth Book* (Theo. LeSieg) is published.

1982 *Hunches in Bunches* is published. Geisel wins an Emmy for the television special *The Grinch Grinches the Cat in the Hat.*

1983 Geisel receives an honorary doctoral degree from John F. Kennedy University.

1984 *The Butter Battle Book*, about warfare, is published. It becomes as controversial as *The Lorax*. Geisel wins a Pulitzer Prize for his contribution to children's literature.

1985 Geisel receives an honorary doctoral degree from Princeton University. The entire graduating class stands and recites *Green Eggs and Ham*, in tribute to Seuss.

1986 *You're Only Young Once!* is published. He receives an honorary doctoral degree from the University of Hartford.

1987 *I Am Not Going to Get Up Today!* is published. He receives an honorary doctoral degree from Brown University, his eighth honorary degree.

1990 *Oh, The Places You'll Go!* is published, and quickly becomes a widely popular high school and college graduation gift.

1991 *Six by Seuss: A Treasury of Dr. Seuss Classics* is published. It includes: *And To Think That I Saw It on Mulberry Street; The 500 Hats of Bartholomew Cubbins; Horton Hatches the Egg; Yertle the Turtle; How the Grinch Stole Christmas* and *The Lorax*.
Theodor Seuss Geisel dies in La Jolla, California, September 24, at 87.

1995 *Daisy-Head Mayzie* is published. It is the only Dr. Seuss book featuring a little girl. *The Secret Art of Dr. Seuss*, pictures that he completed separate from the artwork for his books, is published. Audrey Geisel donates $20 million to the Main Library of the University of California at San Diego. The Library is renamed the Geisel Library.

1996 *My Many Colored Days* is published by Alfred Knopf, Inc. with text by Dr. Seuss and illustrations by Steve Johnson and Lou Fancher. Audrey Geisel donates one million to the library in Theodor Geisel's hometown, Springfield, Mass. A sculpture garden of Dr. Seuss characters is planned for the Library.
Random House publishes *A Hatful of Seuss*, which contains: *If I Ran the Zoo; Sneetches and Other Stories; Horton Hears a Who!; Dr. Seuss' Sleep Book* and *Bartholomew and the Oobleck*.

1997: *Seuss-isms: Wise and Witty Prescriptions for Living from the Good Doctor* is published.

1998: *Horray for Differdoofer Day* is published, based on notes by Seuss left in his study. It is written by Jack Prelutsky and illustrated by Lane Smith.

1999: The Free Press publishes *Dr. Seuss Goes to War: The World War II Editorial Cartoons of Theodor Seuss Geisel.*

Prologue

. . . one of his earliest memories was playing with lion cubs . . .

One of his earliest memories was playing with lion cubs[1] . . . and from his bedroom at night, he often heard the sounds of wild animals howling in the night from their cages in the Springfield Zoo, near his home.

Theodor "Ted" Geisel was born March 2, 1904 in Springfield, Mass., the son of Theodor and Henrietta Geisel. Springfield, 90 miles west of Boston, was then a small, idyllic New England town, with a Mulberry Street and family names like Wickersham, Terwilliger and McElligot. There were parades, industry like the Springfield Armory which made Springfield rifles and companies like the G. and C. Merriam company, the dictionary people.

And there was a large German community. His grandfather, also Theodor Geisel, was a co-owner of the local brewery Kalmbach and Geisel, which locals invariably called "Come back and guzzle."[2]

When he was 13, the United States entered the "Great War," against the Kaiser's Germany and the Geisels, of German extraction, faced a hostile Springfield community and, at the same time, cries grew for liquor regulation. Kalmbach and Geisel had become one of the largest breweries in New England—with production over 300,000 barrels a year—but its entire production would be threatened if beer and liquor were regulated.

It was hard to see which was worse on the Geisels; sauerkraut became "victory cabbage," frankfurters became hot dogs and those of German ancestry and German names were suspect. Anti-liquor crowds in the statehouse in Boston threatened the Geisel brewery. Loyalty to the United States was never an issue in the Geisel house, but they recognized that German name was suspect and a brewery was a risky business.[3]

Theodor's father worked for 35 years to climb the management ladder in the brewery and, in 1920, when he finally became president of the company, by then called Springfield Breweries, the Volstead Act became law and the Geisel brewery became illegal.

Ted's father was at loose ends, with a succession of jobs until 1931, when he became park superintendent, a job which he held for 30 years.[4] The Zoo grew under Geisel's direction and, as the son of the superintendent, Ted remembered later, he played with lion cubs and listened to the howls of the animals at night from his bedroom.

His first book, *And to Think that I Saw it on Mulberry Street* was published in 1937, remembering the Mulberry Street in Springfield and, in 1950, Geisel published *If I Ran the Zoo.*

One

Theodor Geisel, 1904–1927

" . . . when he walked into a room it was like a magician's act. Birds flew out of his hands, and endless bright scarves and fireworks . . ."

For Theodor Geisel, Springfield, Massachusetts, was always large enough to be a city, but small enough to contain all his dreams and memories.

The Springfield, where he was born March 2, 1904, was a growing manufacturing city: The now legendary Indian motorcycle was made there, beginning in 1901. The Indian company also eventually made airplane engines, bicycles, outboard motors and other equipment. It lasted until 1953.

The Smith and Wesson factory was there; as were the Milton Bradley games company; Duryea and Knox automobiles were made there, and watches, machine parts, bicycles, motorcycles, toys, ice skates, roller skates, railroad and trolley cars.[1]

Springfield was served by three railroads: the New York, New Haven & Hartford and the Boston and Albany and as many as two hundred trains pulled into and left Springfield daily.[2]

And there were breweries. His grandfather, also known as

Theodor Geisel (pronounced *GUY*-sell) was born in the German town of Mulhausen in 1840. At 14, he became a jeweler's apprentice and following his apprenticeship, served in the German calvary in Germany's war with Austria and later in battles between the south German states and Prussia. Mustered out in 1867, he left Germany as so many others did and sailed for America.

He settled in Springfield and again took up his craft of jewelry design and manufacturing; four years later he married Christine Schmaelzlea, also a German immigrant and a year after that he became an American citizen.

In 1876, Geisel and Christian Kalmbach who had apprenticed in the German brewing arts, bought a small brewery. They named it Kalmbach and Geisel. Soon everyone who knew it called it "Come Back and Guzzle."[3]

Theodor Geisel, the son of Theodor and Christine Schmaelzlea Geisel, was born in 1979, beside the brewery. By 1891, it was one of the largest breweries in New England. There were twenty-five matched horses to pull the black and gold brewery wagons through the streets of Springfield. Theodor the son eventually joined his Father's brewery.

Henrietta Seuss (pronounced in the German style as *Zoice*. Years later, the name would be corrupted to rhyme with *juice*) was born the daughter of a baker. When Henrietta, the baker's daughter, married Geisel, the brewer's son in 1901, the sally went: "Seuss the baker puts the staff of life in people's mouths; Geisel the brewer takes it out and pours beer there instead, causing the children of drinkers to suffer the pangs of hunger."[4] But it really wasn't true. The Springfield German community, totaling about a thousand, was prosperous and visible—but a minority nonetheless. Its minority status would be much more obvious and at much more at risk later.

Theodor "Ted" Seuss Geisel (who was the third Theodor Geisel, but not saddled with *3rd*, because he was the first Theodor Seuss Geisel) was born in a home at 22 Howard Street, but early in his life the family moved to 74 Fairfield Street, where he would live until he left for college. Geisel remembered the house, its rooms, furniture, smells and sounds for the rest of his life.

His mother, whom the family called Nettie, had sold pies in her Father's bakery before she was married and every night, as Ted and his younger sister Marnie fell asleep, they didn't listen to Nettie telling fairy stories, but rather to her reciting a poem from the bakery:

> Apple, mince, lemon . . .
> Peach, apricot, pineapple . . .
> Blueberry, coconut, custard . . . and *SQUASH!*[5]

Years later, Geisel couldn't keep the drone of a steamship's engine out of his mind; from his childhood he remembered Nettie's pie poem (with the emphasis at the end . . . *and SQUASH!*). More than anyone, Nettie was responsible "for the rhythms in which I write and the urgency with which I do it," he said.[6]

He learned other lessons from Papa Theodor:

> It was Ted's father, Theodor, who imposed discipline, although he rarely raised his voice or his hand. When he grew angry, he turned away and ignored the offender, sometimes for the rest of his life; this was the fate of a cousin he saw almost daily on the Springfield trolley as he went to his office at the brewery. "You will never be sorry," he counseled his son, "for anything you never said." A tall, straight-backed man with black hair and a mustache, he dressed impeccably and looked especially dashing when he donned riding clothes and boots and took his horse for a canter. He drank beer and rye whiskey and smoked cigars, made in Springfield from tobacco grown in the Connecticut Valley. He was an expert marksman who, in 1902, held a world title at two hundred yards. Each morning, as calisthenic discipline, he held his favorite rifle above his head for ten or twelve

> minutes. "My Father had an all-consuming hobby," Ted recalled, "that I always thought was silly and unproductive. It was shooting holes in paper targets. But he was an inspiration. Whatever you do," he told me, "do it to perfection."

Judith and Neil Morgan wrote, in their biography, *Dr. Seuss and Mr. Geisel.*[7]

From Ted's window, at the right rear corner of the second floor of the house, he could see into the country, to a deserted house (neighborhood children thought it was haunted) and, beyond the haunted house (inspiration for the Once-lers house, perhaps?), Ted could hear the sounds and songs of animals in the Springfield Zoo.

When Ted was three, a second sister named after their mother, died of pneumonia, at eighteen months. Ted and his sister Marnie couldn't escape hearing the "terrible sounds of her cough" throughout the house. Her little coffin was displayed in the house and later the family owned a "Pooley cabinet," a narrow New England-made chest in which their Father kept Caruso records. Ted was always haunted by the sheer similarity of the Pooley cabinet to the small narrow coffin which held his sister.

> The cabinet, Ted recalled, was about the size, if you laid it on its side, of my sister's casket. No matter how thrilled I was later by my Father's voice and my mother's accompaniment, I always saw Henrietta in her casket in the place where the Pooley cabinet was.[8]

Ted fell asleep night after night listening to Nettie's pie poem; she discovered that he had a peculiar affinity for rhymes. He knew all the words to "Holy, Holy, Holy, Lord God Almighty!" and memorized this rhyme:

> The great Jehovan speaks to us
> In Genesis and Exodus;
> Leviticus and Numbers, three,
> Followed by Deuteronomy.

Much later Ted admitted he added *three* to make it rhyme; it was surely, his biographers Judith and Neil Morgan wrote, a portent of nonsense to come."[9]

His father was appointed to the Springfield park board in 1909 and Ted entered a whole new world, a world which he never left.

His new domain, Forest Park, was

> flanked by enormous Victorian homes painted in combination of egg-yolk yellow, fire-truck red and peak-soup green. Here Springfield families fished, picnicked and swam in the summer, and went sledding and ice-skating in the winter. Its maze of dead-end paths delighted Ted, as did the bicycle paths. He remembered the first time he saw pink trees and heard their strange name: dogwood.[10]

Decades later, Geisel would be able to remember the colors, the sounds, the animals.

He took a pencil and pad to the Zoo and began to draw the animals that he saw. But his animals were awkward, mis-shapen and, well, tended toward the bizarre. Any normal parents inspecting the drawings of a precocious child might reasonably expect that the drawings would become more accurate and realistic over time and the experiences and age of the child. Ted Geisel's animals remained awkward, mis-shapen and bizarre. Over the years, he *sharpened his skill at making them awkward, mis-shapen and bizarre.*

Consider two other elements of Ted Geisel's world: every night his father came home with the local newspapers and Ted eagerly grabbed the comics. Ted was influenced by George Herriman's

"Crazy Kat" and the other comics in the papers . . . and he was influenced or perhaps hypnotized by his father's inventions, which took on a Rube Goldberg world of their own. His father "invented" a biceps straightening machine; a spring clip to keep flies off the spigots of beer cases and a device which Ted later called a "Silk-Stocking-Back-Seam-Wrong-Detecting Mirror."[11]

But World War One was brewing far over the horizon from idyllic Springfield. The *Lusitania* was torpedoed in 1915 and anti-German sentiment grew. Many senior citizens today remembered when German-style frankfurters suddenly became hot dogs and sauerkraut was patriotically re-named "victory cabbage."

History collided with the Geisels quickly. In 1917, America went to war with Germany and many German-Americans faced increasingly difficult times maintaining a normal life. The Geisel household, along with the 1,200 other German-Americans in Springfield now faced a hostile world: the enemy wasn't a vague shadow from across the Atlantic—for many others in Springfield, and indeed, across the United States, normal American families whose lineage happened to be Germanic who migrated to the United States a generation or two back, were embodiments of the Kaiser. The Hun. The dreaded enemy. The Geisel family did indeed, speak German at home, prayed in German, ate bratwurst, sauerkraut and drank beer. And Ted didn't quite understand why suddenly he had become the neighborhood boy to be picked on.

Prohibition was coming to Springfield, too, and for the Geisels it was even more threatening than the anti-German sentiment.

Theodor Geisel entered Springfield's Central High in the Fall of 1917. One of the courses he chose to take was art. He later explained what happened:

> Our model that day was a milk bottle containing a few scraggly late autumn daisies. I was having a real bad time trying to capture the beauty of this set-up and immortalize it with a hunk of charcoal and a sheet

> of paper. To add to my frustration, my teacher kept fluttering about and giving me hell for turning my drawing board around and working on my picture upside down. "No, Theodor," she said, "Not upside down! There are rules that every artist must abide by. You will never succeed if you break them."

At the end of the class period, Ted Geisel transferred out of that art class and became manager of the high school soccer team. "We lost every game," he later said, "but I was forever free from art-by-the rule book, so I considered it a successful season."[12]

We can almost hear it as a Dr. Seuss rhyme:

No Theodor, No Theodor.
Not upside down, not upside down,
Not even once, not ever more . . .
This I implore, not ever more. . . .

Geisel was doing as other youngsters always do—he was creating a world with no rules. Why shouldn't you, *why shouldn't you, draw upside down?* He was also drawing from the right side of his brain, and making perfect sense while doing so. And when he acknowledged to himself that he would take no more art-by-the-books classes, he permanently freed himself for any further *not upside down* rules.

(It's a wonder that the high school let him transfer out of his art class to become manager of the soccer team . . .)

When his Boy Scout Troop, number 13, sponsored by his Methodist Church, began a war bond drive, Ted went from house to house (perhaps along Mulberry Street) selling war bonds. It helped his family escape the stigma of being *those people*. When Grandfather Theodor, the first brewer, head of young Ted's bond selling, he bought one thousand dollars of bonds, enough to make Ted one of the top ten boy scouts in Springfield in bond sales.

In early May, 1918, Ted and nine other scouts stood on the

stage of the Municipal Auditorium to receive special awards from former President Theodore Roosevelt himself. Roosevelt presented an award personally one-by-one to the nine other boy scouts on the platform, parents beaming in the audience.

When Roosevelt got to Ted, he was inadvertently out of awards. Instead of saving the situation by wit or charm, Roosevelt made the mistake infinitely worse.

"What's this boy doing here?" he loudly asked of adult scout officials. Ted was hustled off the stage, humiliated and mortified and no award was presented.[13]

Years and years later—decades later, as Theodor Geisel or as Dr. Seuss, he remembered the burning, searing embarrassment of his childhood. It became a phobia with him—he would forever be uneasy in crowds and seldom at ease speaking in public. Perhaps it's significant that when he moved and settled in La Jolla, California, he chose a mountaintop where he could be alone, no neighbors crowding in, no one to look at his home and ask *"what's he doing here?"*

(Eventually, it would be easy to say "I can't be at this event—or that event—because I haven't done such things in years." His phobia at facing crowds became a self-fulfilling personality trait.)

Can we listen closely?

(How might Dr. Seuss explain what Ted Geisel could not articulate. . . ?)

I blame it all, I blame it all,
for you see, can't you see,
There was no medal,
no medal at all
that day for me.

In high school he made "B" averages without really trying. He found Latin impossible to comprehend and occasionally cut Latin classes to go to the movies. For the school newspaper,

The Recorder, he wrote one-line quips, known in Springfield as "grinds:"

> It'll just be our luck to be in Latin class
> when they turn back the clocks.

And he drew cartoons, published poetry and satire. Because he contributed so much, he was forced to use a pseudonym: T. S. LeSieg: Geisel spelled backwards. He was to use it again, much later, but it wasn't the first time that pseudonym was used.

When his father played the numbers games, he had to sign the slips so he used T. S. LeSieg. Nettie Geisel didn't particularly mind that her husband played the numbers, but she demanded he use a pseudonym to protect the family's good name.[14]

Prohibition was in. The Eighteenth Amendment—our grand exercise in national self-control—became legal in January, 1919. But grandfather Geisel, the first *brewmeister*, didn't live to see it; he died just before Prohibition was enacted.

Kalmbach and Geisel ("Come Back and Guzzle") had grown and merged and became Liberty Breweries and eventually it became Springfield Breweries, one of the largest in New England. Ted's father's career had grown with the brewery and he had become president. Just before Prohibition. Then he was out of a job.

Geisel starred in a minstrel show which he wrote; he appeared in "Twelfth Night" and was the "grind and joke editor" for his senior high school yearbook, *Pnalka*. With the advice and encouragement of his English teacher, who had graduated from Dartmouth two years previously, Geisel applied to Dartmouth and was accepted.

He chose Dartmouth because a teacher he liked at Central High, Edwin A. "Red" Smith had graduated from Dartmouth two years earlier. As Geisel remembered it, years later:

> The reason why so many kids went to Dartmouth at that particular time from the Springfield high school was probably Red Smith, a young English teacher who, rather

than being just another English teacher was one of the gang—a real stimulating guy who probably was responsible for my starting to write.

I think many kids were excited by this fellow. . . . And I think when time came to go to college, we all said, "Let's go where Red Smith went."[15]

His classmates voted him Class Artist and Class Wit, but in group pictures he stood in the back row, tall and unsmiling.[16]

And, while waiting to attend Dartmouth, Geisel discovered the writer Hilaire Belloc (1870–1953). In an introduction to a reprint edition of *Cautionary Tales*, Sally Holmes Holtze writes:

> Readers of the Introduction might understandably assume that Belloc was a children's book writer, but in fact his humorous writing was only a minute part of what he published in his 83 years. Belloc was born in France in 1870 and became a British subject in 1902. After graduating from Balliol College, Oxford, where he was a Brackenbury History Scholar, he began writing short pieces for publication in magazines. He was astonishing prolific as an essayist, novelist, historian, poet, translator, and editor and wrote well over 100 books; yet he was always troubled by debt and poverty. He was also a fascinating character, a devout Roman Catholic who doggedly applied his religion to every aspect of his life, including his political views, and this devotion was a handicap to his career. Belloc wrote, "I am used to Insult, as I combine in one person . . . A)Poverty. B) Papistry. C)Pugnacity. Any one of three can just swim, but when all three come together the victim sinks" (from *Yesterday's Authors of Books for Children*, 1977). Indeed, he was a difficult man to deal with; he was so unpredictable in temperament that a friend describes him as "ruder and more courteous, kinder and yet more pugnacious

> than any man I have ever met" (*Selected Cautionary Verses*, Penguin Puffin edition, 1964). Despite any problems he felt other people had with his Catholicism—he complained that his historical perspective wasn't what either Catholics *or* Protestants wanted to teach, and he was told that his religious fervor would prevent him from being elected to a professorship at Glasgow University in 1899—he received many honors in his lifetime. He served in Parliament from 1906 to 1910; he was honored by the Pope; he had honorary degrees from Glasgow University and from Dublin University. Belloc was a passionate man of great knowledge, who worked unceasingly. And he was a man who understood and liked children.
>
> He knew children's tastes for the kind of incredible disasters that occur in *Cautionary Tales*, and he produced these calamities in just the right exaggerated style, so that children could never take the punishments seriously. Because of his skill, his humor, and his art, readers of *Cautionary Tales* continue to find the book memorable and enjoyable.[17]

Geisel was enchanted by *The Bad Child's Book of Beasts: Verses*, first published in England in 1896. The first printing sold out in four days. Belloc published *More Beasts (for Worse Children)* in 1897 and *Cautionary Tales for Children: Designed for the Admonition of Children Between the Ages of Eight and Fourteen Years*, was published in 1907. Geisel memorized chunks of Belloc poems like:

Matilda,
Who Told Lies, and was Burned to Death.

They galloped, roaring through the Town,
"Matilda's House is Burning Down!"

Inspired by British Cheers and Loud
Proceeding from the Frenzied Crowd,
They ran their ladders through a score
Of windows on the Ball Room Floor;
And took Peculiar Pains to Souse
The Pictures up and down the House,[18]

It was Belloc, Ted said, years later, who introduced him to the hypnotic joys of rhyme.[19] And, we can assume, to Belloc rhyme schemes like:

And took Peculiar Pains to Souse
The Pictures up and down the House.

Geisel surely realized that Belloc's poems were satires of pure and oh-so-dreary moralistic rhymes of the day, just as Lewis Carroll's poem "You are Old, Father William," from *Alice In Wonderland* is a parody. The original (with the same title) was written by Robert Southey (1774–1843):

You are old, father William, the
  young man cried,
the few locks which are left you
  are grey;
You are hale, father William, a
  hearty old man;
Now tell me the reason I pray. . . .

Lewis Carroll's version:

You are old, father William, the
  young man said,
And your hair has become very white;
And yet you increasingly stand on your head—
  Do you think, at your age, it is right?"[20]

Sally Holmes Holtze writes:

> How could children go back to the plodding verses that condescended to them in such tiresome moralizing, after they had met the girl in "Rebecca, Who slammed Doors for Fun and Perished Miserably"? The very language of Belloc's tales seemed to inform children that the stilted phraseology of their previous books had been a sham.[21]

Readers need not know the original to understand how Belloc was using parody, she says, just as readers did not need to know the Robert Southey original to enjoy how Lewis Carroll mocked the lessons of age in "You are Old, Father William."

Children clearly understood the rollicking rhymes and phrases—the freedom—of Belloc's style. And he understood children's tastes for "incredible disasters."

They were lessons not lost on Ted Geisel.

He began classes at Dartmouth College, four hours north of Springfield, in the fall of 1921. Although Geisel's father was now unemployed when the brewery sat idle during the Depression, there was enough money from Grandfather Geisel to allow Ted to pay Dartmouth's tuition, then $250. annually.

Fraternity pledge week came and went and although Geisel made no real efforts toward fraternity life, he was surprised and perhaps chagrined when no offer at all came from any fraternity. Months later, Geisel discovered that his dark hair and sharp nose made Dartmouth fraternity members believe that he was Jewish and thus effectively blackballed from fraternity life.

But shortly after Pledge Week, Geisel discovered the *Jack-o-Lantern*, the Dartmouth humor magazine and he turned to the *Jacko* (as the staff called it) with relief and enthusiasm. And he quickly found a friend, Norman Maclean, son of a Presbyterian minister from Montana. Maclean would eventually become a professor of English at the University of Chicago and, later in his professional career, publish *A River Runs Through It*, now considered a classic.

Geisel began cartooning for the *Jacko*; one of his first cartoons showed a co-ed with a short skirt and an unnaturally large leg. The cartoon bore the title: "The Fatted Calf."[22]

His habits echo those of thousands, or perhaps hundreds of thousands of young men in college, then or now. A college friend, Frederick "Pete" Blodgett said, of him:

> He never had any money but he never spent much. He was always raising hell and laughing a lot and didn't study worth a damn.[23]

His best grade at Dartmouth during his freshman year was an "A" in first semester German (an automatic since he spoke German at home), but even that slipped to a "B" during the spring semester.

His sophomore grades weren't much better. In Botany, he only survived when his professor Arthur H. Chivers, promised him and Blodgett a raise of one letter grade if they memorized four tree species in Latin. (Geisel had spent hours in class sketching, rather than taking notes. Blodgett's notes weren't much helpful.) They made a game of the memorization and both got a "C," up from their previous "D" work in Botany.[24]

During his second year at Dartmouth, fraternities which had ignored him, now rushed him. Geisel joined Sigma Phi Episilon but was an indifferent frat member during his years at Dartmouth, although he remembered the Sig Ep rituals throughout his life.

Geisel found another importance influence in the Dartmouth English Department:

> . . . my big inspiration for writing there was Ben Pressey (W. Benfield Pressey . . .). He was (as) important to me in college as Red Smith was in high school.

> He seemed to like the stuff I wrote. He was very informal, and he had little seminars at his house (plus a very beautiful wife who served us cocoa). In between sips of cocoa, we students read our trash out loud.
>
> He's the only person I took any creative writing courses from ever, anywhere, and he was very kind and encouraging.
>
> I remember being in a big argument at one of Ben's seminars. I maintained that subject matter wasn't as important as method. . . .
>
> To prove my point, I did a book review of the Boston and Maine Railroad timetable. As I remember, nobody in the class thought it was funny—except Ben and me.[25]

Geisel also had a memory for cartoons, situations, phrases. "When I went to college," he remembered, "it was a campy thing to say, 'Oh, the places you'll go! The people you'll meet!'"[26]

Dr. Seuss published *Oh! The Places You'll Go!*, a *paean* to high school and college graduates everywhere, over six decades later, in 1990.

At Dartmouth, in his junior year, he finally made the mental leap of joining pictures and text:

> This was the year I discovered the excitement of "marrying" words to pictures.
>
> I began to get it through my skull that words and pictures were Yin and Yan. [sic] I began thinking that words and pictures, married, might possibly produce a progeny more interesting than either parent.
>
> It took me almost a quarter of a century to find the proper way to get my words and pictures married. At Dartmouth I couldn't even get them engaged.[27]

Norman Maclean and Geisel developed a fanciful technique for collaboration:

> Norman and I had a rather peculiar method of creating literary gems, Geisel recalled.[28] Hunched behind his typewriter, he would bang out a line of words.
>
> Sometimes he'd tell me what he'd written, sometimes not. But, then, he'd always say, "The next line's yours." And, always, I'd supply it.
>
> That may have made for rough reading. But it was great sport writing.

As others discovered, writing and editing a college newspaper or magazine was a better education than mere college classes.

> My big desire . . . was to run that magazine. If Mac (Norman Maclean) hadn't picked me as his successor my whole life at college would have been a failure.[29]

He was elected editor in mid-May, 1924. In the summer prior to his senior year, the Geisel family financial crisis eased, as his father sold a piece of Springfield property he had owned for six months—for a thirty thousand dollar profit. But Geisel senior still had no real job; he had been elected to the Springfield Park Board, but that was almost an honorary title. Only later, in 1931, when he was appointed Park Superintendent, did he earn a real paycheck.[30]

In his senior year, Geisel was one of twenty elected to Casque and Gauntlet, the Dartmouth senior honorary. One member, Kenneth Montgomery remembered Geisel:

> He was not gregarious in the sense of hail-fellow-well-met; there was no sense of self-importance about him. But when he walked into a room it was like a magician's act. Birds flew out of his hands, and endless bright scarves and fireworks. Everything became brighter, happier, funnier. And he didn't try. Everything Ted did seemed to be a surprise, even to him.[31]

But, at the same time, Casque and Gauntlet members voted him "least likely to succeed."

But one Saturday night in April, 1925, Geisel got caught after sharing some bootleg liquor with friends; the Dartmouth Dean demanded that he write to his parents explaining that he was on probation. And although his name remained in the magazine, he was forbidden to contribute to the *Jack-O-Lantern*. But Geisel was not banned from the magazine's offices, so he continued to contribute, using a variety of pseudonyms, including L. Burbank (a bow to Arthur H. Chivers, his Botany professor) and Thomas Mott Osborn, who was then warden of Sing Sing, the infamous prison in New York.[32]

Geisel also used the pen-name Seuss.

He approached graduation with no career in sight, no job on the horizon, no plans, and—and no real ambition to do anything. But when his Father asked what he was to do, Geisel grandly said that he was going to win a scholarship—a Campbell Fellowship from Dartmouth—to attend Oxford University, in England.

Geisel's father took the news to the editor of *The Springfield Union*, who lived across the street from the Geisel's. The news was promptly printed. Geisel remembered that it was on the front page:[33]

GEISEL WINS FELLOWSHIP TO GO TO OXFORD

Then Ted was forced to tell his father that he had *applied* to receive the Campbell Scholarship, but didn't get it.

Ted didn't receive any punishment from his father, nor even a lecture—his father's disapproving silence was enough. Geisel the elder then admitted that since Ted had announced he would be attending Oxford, then he must attend. Readers of *The Springfield Union* and friends of the family would forget about the scholarship.

Looking back on his career at Dartmouth, Ted said:

> English and writing was my major, but I think that's a mistake for anybody. That's teaching you the mechanics of getting water out of a well that may not exist.[34]

True advice, ignored by thousands of English majors everywhere.

Geisel spent the summer after his graduation working for *The Springfield Union*, doing miscellaneous work. When the *Lowell*, Mass. *Courier-Citizen* celebrated happy birthday with a rhymed couplet to the Governor, Ted topped that in the *Union*:

> We'll go you just one better
> (*The Springfield Union* says)
> And wish a happy birthday
> to Calvin Coolidge, Pres.[35]

Theodor Geisel reached Lincoln College, Oxford University in October, 1925; British academia was worlds away from Geisel's safe haven of Dartmouth. He arrived just in time for the election of a student as Guardian of the College Cat.[36]

Again, Geisel was the outsider; he was a Yank in a British University and he was of German extraction in a land which had just fought Germany bitterly and had not yet forgotten World War One. So he read and studied by himself. Eventually he found other outsiders, including a young lady named Mirabel who had spent her earlier years in "the India of the Raj, where Papa wore a pith helmet and shoulder straps." When Geisel and Mirabel staged a dramatic love affair for a fellow student with a movie camera—with the Dean of the College, J.A.R. Munro looking on from a distance—Munro never spoke to Geisel again.[37]

Geisel found much of Oxford life trivial, tedious or bizarre. He was treated as an underling in the dining halls even though he was older than many of the British students. He did not participate in rugby, didn't like the British food, didn't care much for the beer drinking contests in the dining halls, didn't like the hours and the classes. Perhaps most of all he didn't like the classes.

Oxford was very, very pompous and deliberately so. Oxford had centuries of pomposity to live up to and in the 1920s, was doing nothing to change. Ted Geisel was leery of, or alternatively, bemused by pomposity.

But instead of keeping a diary of his thoughts, emotions and reactions, Geisel kept a sketchbook.

His future life lay literally in the margins.

He had to attend lectures:

> on Geoffrey Chaucer (whom he called Jeff), Shakespeare and Milton. Among its sixty-eight pages are a few with words only, but most are thronged with pen-and-ink Seussian cartoons. Sometimes a sketch erupted from the subject of the lecture, but any Oxford don confronted with the result would have felt ready to suggest to the young American (as one eventually did) that his future lay elsewhere. Beside his notes in Anglo-Saxon for Beginners stands a drooling milk cow burdened with a sagging udder, rams' horns and angels wings. A pair of baroque daggers decorates the margin, along with a coat of arms from which a trapped bird struggles to free itself. On the same page as desultory notes on Keats' odes, three dogs move in terror across high wires, a small chicken wears a windmill for a tail, and a despondent devil contemplates his failures. As Ted noted dutifully that the translation of the holy Bible was the greatest literary achievement in the reign of King James he was also deep at work creating a Chaplinesque clown, slumping beneath the weight of military epaulettes and a crown from which grew a soaring cross. In a lecture by Emile Legouis, an authority on William Wordsworth and Jonathan Swift,

> Ted sketched himself, sinking into deep water, with the caption "Mr. Legouis attempts once more to attract my attention in a lecture entitled. . . ?" Among his notes on Dryden, a black-faced Cupid appears with a quiver of arrows. So does the profile of a chic young woman wearing a snug cloche. "You hoo," cries a male profile as he peers up the loose-leaf binder at the cloche.[38]

And his future wife literally read his life through the margins of his sketchbook.

Helen Marion Palmer, a graduate of Wellesley, was almost six years older than Geisel. She had come to Oxford a year earlier, after teaching English in Brooklyn for three years.

She watched Geisel illustrate Milton's *Paradise Lost* in his own way.

Geisel remembered Uriel:

> While I was at Oxford I illustrated a great hunk of *Paradise Lost*.
>
> With the imagery of *Paradise Lost*, Milton's sense of humor failed him in a couple of places. I remember one line, "Thither came the angel Uriel, sliding down a sunbeam."
>
> I illustrated that: Uriel had a long locomotive oil can and was greasing the sunbeam as he descended, to lessen the friction on his coccyx.[39]

> "You're crazy to be a professor," (Helen) said, after a class.
>
> "What you really want to do is draw." And, looking at his sketchbook, said, "that's a very fine flying cow."[40]

Any young woman who could appreciate Uriel and his oil can and the flying cow and the drooling cow with a sagging udder, rams' horns and wings, a Chaplinesque clown, dogs walking along high wires, the chicken with a windmill for a tail, the black-faced Cupid, the young woman wearing the snug cloche and the leering male in the margins, was for him.

Theodor Geisel fell in love with Helen Palmer and just as quickly she fell in love with him.

The two became inseparable; Geisel knew that first year students were not allowed to own cars or other motor vehicles, but Helen wasn't a first year student. So after Christmas break, they pooled their money and bought a motorcycle, with a sidecar. Ted appropriated some Oxford ducks and maintained the fantasy that he was a deliveryman, with live ducks in tow.

By the end of the first year, Geisel knew as well as Helen that Oxford wasn't for him. And he wasn't for Oxford.

> My tutor was A.J. Carlyle, the nephew of the great frightening Thomas Carlyle. I was surprised to see him alive. He was surprised to see me in any form.
>
> He was the oldest man I've ever seen riding a bicycle. I was the only man he'd ever seen who never should have come to Oxford.
>
> This brilliant scholar had taken a "First" in every school in Oxford, excepting medicine, without studying. Every year, up to his eighties, he went up for a different "First," just for the hell of it.
>
> Patiently, he had me write essays and listened to me read them, in the usual manner of the Oxford tutorial system. But he realized I was getting stultified in English schools.
>
> I was bogged down with old High German and Gothic and stuff of that sort, in which I have no interest whatsoever—and I don't think anybody really should.
>
> Well, he was a great historian and he quickly discovered that I didn't know *any* history. Somehow or other I got through high school and Dartmouth without taking one history course.

> He very correctly told me I was ignorant, and he was the man who suggested that I do what I finally did: just travel around Europe with a bundle of high school history books and visit the places I was reading about—go to the museums and look at pictures and read as I went. That's what I finally did.[41]

Years later, Geisel clearly remembered the final academic straw. . . . He had a don (Sir Oliver Onions) who had produced a variorum edition of Shakespeare and who was chiefly interested in punctuational differences in Shakespearean texts:

> That was the man who really drove me out of Oxford. I'll never forget his two hour lecture on the punctuation of *King Lear*.
>
> He had dug up all of the old folios, as far back as he could go. Some had more semi-colons than commas. Some had more commas than periods. Some had no punctuation at all.
>
> For the first hour and a half he talked about the first two pages in *King Lear*, lamenting the fact that modern people would never comprehend the true essence of Shakespeare, because it's punctuated badly these days.
>
> It got unbelievable. I got up, went back to my room and started packing.[42]

Ted and Helen spent some months in Europe, beginning in the summer of 1926 (Helen chose to remain in Oxford to complete her degree); he met his parents and his sister Marnie. They toured Switzerland, Munich, Nuremberg, Dresden and Berlin. They stopped in Mulhausen, to honor the memory of the Geisels who emigrated to Springfield. In the hamlet of Kleinschwarzenbach, they hosted a dinner for the Seusses and sixty-seven people attended.[43] His family finally returned to the United States and Geisel stayed in Paris.

Geisel recognized that he wasn't exactly in the wave of American expatriate literature of the 1920s; one night in Paris, he caught a glimpse of Ernest Hemingway:

> . . . a worldly man of twenty-seven, smoking a pipe and writing from time to time on a thick pad. "What he was writing, I never knew," Ted admitted. "I was scared . . . to walk over and ask him, lest he ask me what I was writing. I was a twenty-two-year-old kid writing knock-kneed limericks about goats and cheese and other stuff that I couldn't sell. He was probably writing *A Farewell to Arms*."[44]

Geisel met Helen for a short tour of Vienna, then returned to Paris where he gave academics one more try. At Oxford, he had met Emile Legouis, an expert on Wordsworth and Swift. And Geisel had admired *Gulliver's Travels*.

> At Oxford I went to a lecture (I was very interested in Jonathan Swift) by the great Emile Legouis. Although he was a Frenchman, he was the greatest Swift authority in the world at that time.
>
> He talked to me at the end of the lecture and began selling me on going to study with him at the Sorbonne. And, after I left Oxford, I did so.
>
> I registered at the Sorbonne, and I went over to his house to find out exactly what he wanted me to do.
>
> He said, "I have a most interesting assignment which should only take you about two years to complete." He said that nobody had ever discovered anything that Jonathan Swift wrote from the ages of 16 and a half to 17.
>
> He said that I should devote two years to finding out whether he *had* written anything. If he had, I could analyze what he wrote as my D.Phil. thesis. Unfortunately, if he hadn't written anything, I wouldn't get my doctorate.

I remember leaving his charming home and walking straight to the American Express Company and booking myself a passage on a cattle boat to Corsica.

There I proceeded to paint donkeys for a month. Then, I proceeded with Carlyle's idea and began living all around the Continent, reading history books, going to museums and drawing pictures.

I remember a long time period in which I drew nothing but gargoyles. They were easier than Mona Lisas.[45]

Which was not exactly true. He journeyed to Italy and met Helen, who was touring with her Mother. He visited Florence, witnessed the growth of the Mussolini movement and, with Helen, saw Michelangelo's David. Helen's Mother appeared shocked. She would have been happier "if all art, including Raphael's pre-puberty cheribs, wore jockstraps," Geisel said.[46]

He produced some drawings based on what he saw, which he called his "Roman and Florentine Period":

These fractured bits of Roman history include a Seussian version of Romulus and Remus, a group of vestal virgins on the forum, and a dragon, drawn directly from the central monster in *Perseus Frees Andromeda* by Piero di Cosimo in the Uffizi Gallery, Florence. This was the last time that art history was to intrude on Geisel's work.[47]

He also tried to write a novel:

While floating around Europe trying to figure out what I wanted to do with my life, I decided at one point that I would be the Great American Novelist. And so I sat down and wrote the Great American Novel.

It turned out to be not so great, so I boiled it down into the Great American Short Story. It wasn't very great in that form either.

> Two years later I boiled it down once more and sold it as a two-line joke to *Judge* (magazine).[48]

Finally, Geisel sailed home, presumably full of Europe, and especially full of academia. He arrived in New York in February, 1927, with no graduate degree, no job, no prospects for a job, no *talent* for a job. He returned to Springfield and drew at his Father's desk. The animals he drew were the animals he had always drawn—odd, mis-shapen, bizarre—but animals which were somehow comical and entertaining. They weren't frightening, just odd. Helen told her relatives and others that his animals were "the sort you'd like to take home to meet the family."[49]

He journeyed to New York and knocked on doors all over Manhattan. In a letter to Dartmouth friend Whitney Campbell he said:

> I have tramped all over this bloody town and been tossed out of Boni and Liveright, Harcourt Brace, Paramount Pictures, Metro-Goldwyn, three advertising agencies, *Life*, *Judge*, and three public conveniences . . . [58]

He returned to Springfield, dismayed. Again he aimed for *Life*[51] magazine and *The New Yorker*.

Finally, one day, the mailman left an envelope from *The Saturday Evening Post*. Geisel had sent them a drawing of two American tourists riding camels and comparing their journey to Lawrence of Arabia. It was his first professional sale. *The Post* had sent a check for twenty-five dollars. When it ran, the by-line said: Seuss.[52]

Two

1927–1939

The drone of the Kungsholm's engine became the driving force of Dr. Seuss's career.

With that thin blade of success of his one cartoon in *The Saturday Evening Post,* and one thousand dollars, his profits from working on the *Jack-o-Lantern* at Dartmouth, Geisel moved to New York. He shared a dingy apartment over a nightclub with a friend, John C. Rose, and this time, Geisel had better luck in New York.

He knew that his best chances as a cartoonist lay with *Judge* magazine (Harold Ross had left *Judge* in 1925 to start *The New Yorker*). Geisel made an appointment with the editor, and promptly got a job as writer and artist (read cartoonist). His salary was seventy-five dollars a week and on that salary he and Helen Palmer could get married. (Some relatives thought that Geisel and Palmer had already been married in Europe. Years later, when he was asked about any such European wedding, Geisel only smiled.[1])

They delayed their wedding because Ted's sister Marnie was due to have her first baby and they didn't want Ted's parents to miss one happy event because of the other. On November 29, 1927, four weeks after her daughter Peggy was born, Theodor

Geisel and Helen Palmer were married in the living room of her home. He was twenty-three; she twenty-nine.

Back at *Judge*, after an Atlantic City honeymoon, Geisel contributed his first cartoon as a staff member. It showed two unicyclists, on very tall unicycles, one speaking to the other. "And to think that today I could have been the wife of a six-day bicycle racer, if I hadn't listened to your rot about Higher Art."[2]

Only weeks later, Geisel added "Dr." to his by-line Seuss, explaining it made up for the doctoral degree he never got in Oxford. Much later, he also explained that he "saved" his own name to use as the by-line on the novel he intended to write. He never used his own name again and he never really attempted to write the Great American Novel.

Quickly after using "Seuss," he used "Dr. Theophrastus Seuss" for an on-going *Judge* feature, "Boids and Beasties, A Department for Indefatigable Naturalists." Some of the creatures for this series were taken almost line-for-line out of the margins of his Oxford notebook.

He used a tipsy elephant to illustrate a feature, "Quaffing with the Pachyderms: Why I Prefer the West Side Speakeasies" (it easily could have been the precursor of Horton the elephant, hero of *Horton Hatches the Egg* and *Horton Hears a Who*[3]) and he began a series, "being ye inside dope on King Arthur's Court translated from Merlin's memoirs." His experiences in the cloistered halls of Oxford gave him more than enough images for that series.

> Among Ted's first fan letters at *Judge* was a curt note from a condemned murderer on death row in Huntsville, Texas, written on the eve of his electrocution. "If your stuff is the kind of thing they're publishing nowadays," the prisoner took the time to write, "I don't so much mind leaving." Ted was enraptured with the letter and kept it at his desk throughout his long life, always feigning fear of running into the felon, whose sentence had been commuted at the last minute.[4]

Critic George Jean Nathan was on the staff of *Judge*, and S. J. Perelman was in the magazine as was Pare Lorentz, who wrote film reviews, but the new *New Yorker* judged *Judge* its main competition and advertisers began deserting *Judge* for *The New Yorker*. Geisel had to take a pay cut to fifty dollars a week.

He clearly remembered those days at *Judge*:

> And the *next* week they instituted another fiscal policy (I was getting a little bit worried by this time) in which they dispensed with money entirely and paid contributors with due bills. "Due bills . . ?"
>
> *Judge* had practically no advertising. And the advertisers it attracted seldom paid for the ads with money; they paid the magazine with due bills. And that's what we, the artists and writers, ended up with in lieu of salary.
>
> For instance: a hundred dollars, the only way for me to get the hundred dollars was to go down to the Hotel Traymore in Atlantic City and move into a hundred-dollar suite.
>
> So, Helen and I spent many weeks of our first married year in sumptuous suites in Atlantic City—where we didn't want to be at all.
>
> Under the due-bill system I got paid once, believe it or not, in a hundred cartons of Barbasol Shaving Cream. Another time I got paid in 13 gross of Little Gem nail clippers.
>
> Looking back on it, it wasn't really so bad, because I didn't have to balance any checkbooks—or file any income tax.
>
> How can you file an income tax when you're being paid in cases of White Rock soda?[5]

He also said . . .

> . . . I sort of loved trading my stuff for their stuff. I was happier in one way under the barter system than I've ever been since. When you get paid in money, it leads to accountants and lawyers.[6]

Geisel always claimed that serendipity played a large part in his career. And when *Judge* was faltering, a financial godsend was near.

In the late 1920s, well before air conditioning, families had to keep the windows or screens open, and use flyswatters, flypaper or bug sprays to keep the inside insect population down.

> I'd been working for *Judge* about four months when I drew this accidental cartoon which changed my whole life. It was an insect gag.
>
> It was a picture of a knight who had gone to bed. He had stacked his armor beside the bed. Here was this covered canopy over the bed, and a tremendous dragon was sort of nuzzling him.
>
> He looked up and said, "Darn it all, Another Dragon. And just after I'd sprayed the whole castle with . . ."
>
> With *what*? I wondered.
>
> There were two well-known insecticides. One was Flit and one was Fly-Tox. So, I tossed a coin. It came up heads, for Flit.
>
> So, the caption read, " . . . another dragon. And just after I'd sprayed the whole castle with Flit."
>
> Here's where luck comes in.
>
> Very few people ever bought *Judge*. It was continually in bankruptcy—and everybody else was bankrupt, too.
>
> But one day the wife of Lincoln L. Cleaves, who was the account executive at the McCann-Erickson advertising agency, failed to get an appointment at her favorite hairdresser's, and went to a second-rate

> hairdresser's, where they had second-rate magazines around.
>
> She opened *Judge* while waiting to get her hair dressed, and she found this picture. She ripped it out of the magazine, put it in her reticule, took it home, bearded her husband with it, and said, "Lincoln, you've got to hire this young man; it's the best Flit ad I've ever seen.
>
> He said, "Go away." He said, "you're my wife and you're to have nothing to do with my business."
>
> So she finally pestered him for about two weeks and finally he said, "All right, I'll have him in and buy one picture."
>
> He had me in. I drew one picture, which I captioned "Quick Henry, The Flit!"—and it was published.
>
> Then, they hired me to do two more—and 17 years later I was still doing them.
>
> The only good thing Adolph Hitler did in starting World War II was that he enabled me to join the Army and finally stop drawing "Quick Henry the Flit!"
>
> I had drawn them by the millions—newspaper ads, magazine ads, booklets, window displays, 24-sheet posters, even "Quick Henry, the flit!" animated cartoons. Flit was pouring out of my ears and beginning to itch me.[7]

The Flit campaign, all seventeen years, entered America's vernacular, just as other phrases would, throughout the years. Geisel drew situation after situation involving Flit. In one cartoon, a prisoner is surrounded by insects during a prison break; in another, a genie is also surrounded by bugs during a seance. A song was written about the phrase; Flit sales grew wildly. The only other comparable campaign was the Burma Shave four-line highway signs.[8] Flit insured Geisel's financial security, year after year.

And it allowed Geisel very considerable freedom of time:

> My contract with the Standard Oil Company was an exclusive one and forbade me from doing an awful lot of stuff.
>
> Flit being seasonal, its ad campaign was only run during the summer months. I'd get my work done in about three months, and I had all this spare time and nothing to do.
>
> They let me work for magazines, because I'd already established that. But it crimped future expansion into other things.[9]

The Geisels were so comfortable, from the Flit income, they were able to tour Greece during the spring of 1928. They moved into a better apartment and, one morning while shaving, Geisel thought of a party they attended the night before. He completed this poem.

> Mrs. Van Bleck
> Of the Newport Van Blecks
> Is so goddam rich
> She has gold-plated sex
> Whereas Miggles and Mitzi
> And Blitzie and Sue
> Have the commonplace thing
> And it just has to do.[10]

Geisel began selling cartoons to *Liberty* and *Life* (the old *Life*, not the Luce *Life*). The first *Life* was the one that was *intentionally* funny, one New York wag said.[11]

To celebrate their first anniversary, the Geisels took a train to southern California, at the suggestion of John Rose, Geisel's former New York City roommate. There, they were impressed by La Jolla, a small village between the ocean and San Diego. Everything in La Jolla was a marked contrast to their previous lives in New York: they had the seascapes, fresh air; even in the winter there were swimmers in the surf. They saw plants in wild profusion they had never seen before. It had a Mediterranean look and feel. Much of the architecture was Mediterranean/Spanish. They were enchanted by it all. And they quickly resolved, somehow, to move to La Jolla.

Geisel became fascinated by words; how they were spelled, how they were pronounced; how they *behaved*. Readers of *Judge* shared his fascination with *ough* words, in his feature, titled "Ough! Ough! Or Why I Believe in Simplified Spelling":

"The Tough Coughs As He Ploughs the Dough":

It was forty-five years ago, when I first came to America as a young Roumanian student of divinity, that I first met the evils of the "ough" words. Strolling one day in the country with my fellow students, I saw a tough, coughing as he ploughed a field which (being quite near-sighted) I mistook for pie dough.

Assuming that all "ough" words were pronounced the same, I casually remarked, "The tuff cuffs as he pluffs the duff!"

"Sacriledge," shrieked my devout companions, "He is cursing in Roumanian! . . ."

"Mr. Hough, Your Bough is in the Trough"

The ministry being closed to me, I then got a job as a chore boy on the farm of an eccentric Mr. Hough, who happened to spend most of his time in the bough of a tree overhanging a trough. I was watering a colt one morning when I noticed that Mr. Hough's weight had forced the bough down into the water. "Mr. Hoo!" I shouted, "Your Boo is in the Troo!" Thinking I was speaking lightly of his wife, Mr. Hough fired me on the spot.

"Enough, Enough! I'm Through!"

So I drifted into the prize ring. But here again the curse of the *oughs* undid me. One night in the Garden, I was receiving an unmerciful trouncing from a mauler twice my size. Near the end of the sixth round I could stand it no longer. I raised my feeble hand in surrender. "Eno! Eno!" I gulped. "I'm thuff." "Insults like that I take from no man!" bellowed my opponent, and he slugged me into a coma! Something snapped! . . . a maddening flash . . . and all became black. Fifteen years later I awoke to find myself the father of three homely daughters named Xough, Yough and Zough. I had become a through-going Augho-maniac.[12]

A collection of schoolroom gaffes was published in England under the title *Schoolboy Howlers*. The Viking Press bought the U.S. publication rights and changed the title to *Boners*. Geisel was paid a set rate (but no royalties) to illustrate the book, published in 1931. It was a surprise best seller; and teachers sent in their own best examples of school room *faux pas*. The sequel, *More Boners*, was also published before the end of 1931. Geisel began to think:

That was a big depression year. And although by Depression standards I was adequately paid a flat fee for illustrating these best-sellers, I was money-worried. The two books were booming and I was not.

This is the point when I first began to realize that if I hoped to succeed in the book world, I'd have to write as well as draw.[13]

He was also encouraged by a review in *American News*:

offhand . . . we should have said this would be a flop. But the inimitable illustrations of the renowned Dr.

> Seuss, of *Judge, Life* and Flit fame, are not unlikely to put this over. They are simply swell.

He subsequently received a second endorsement from the same publication:

> Seuss puts more naive satisfaction into the face of a cat, more passion into the face of a Cleopatra, more anticipation into the face of a Mark Anthony, than many other cartoonists could do if brought together in the same speakeasy.

So he wrote and illustrated a children's ABC book, full of Seussian animals, with seventeen different colors of blue and three colors of red. He took it to publishers Bobbs Merrill, Viking Press, Simon and Schuster and others . . . where it was promptly rejected. He abandoned it.[15]

But Flit begat Esso.

And pictures begat poems.

For Flit he wrote (about the knight and the dragon):

> If Flit can knock
> *this* monster stiff
> Mere bugs and such
> won't last one *whiff*!

And they even generated three rare Seussian books of advertising cartoons: *Flit Cartoons As They Have Appeared in Magazines Throughout the Country* (Vol. 1, 1929 and Vol. 2, 1930) and *Another Big Flit! Year* (1931).

The cartoons were all the same; neither Flit nor Esso, nor later, Shaeffer Bock Beer, nor Ford, nor Atlas Products, nor New Departure Bearings, nor NBC Radio, or Holly Sugar ever asked Geisel to change the Seuss drawings. They didn't carry a Seuss-by-line; they didn't have to. Seuss creatures and Seuss rhymes were becoming nationally recognized. For Esso, a series of panels with monkeys, dragons and such:

> Foil the Moto-raspus!
>
> Foil the Zero-doccus!
>
> Foil the Karbo-nockus![16]

Geisel was doing quite, quite well during the days of the Great Depression.

One day in the early 1930s, Geisel got a package at his apartment door: his father sent him a heavy slab of stone . . . imbedded in it: a dinosaur footprint eleven inches wide and sixteen inches long. The Geisels couldn't find a good place for it—they tripped over it and stubbed their toes on it. For a while Geisel thought he'd hang it on the wall for visitors to kiss, like an ancient Blarney Stone, but his wife didn't go for that.[17] It was a perfect Seussian gift: it reminded him of the minuteness of man in the vast time of the universe and he kept it with him, move after move; it took his mind back to prehistoric days, where he could visualize dinosaurs thumping and thundering about and then it would be a very slight jump—or no jump at all—to think of far different Seussian creatures.

It also taught—and retaught—him a valuable lesson:

> It keeps me from getting conceited. Whenever I think I'm pretty good, I just go out and look at it. Half the people I show it to think I've made it myself.[18]

In 1935, Standard Oil, which produced Flit, asked Geisel to work on another campaign, leading to his long "Naval Career." As he remembered it:

They had a product called Esso marine, a lubricating oil for boats, and they didn't have a lot of money to spend on advertising.

They decided to see what we could do with public relations. So, Harry Bruno, a great PR man, Ted Cook and Verne Carrier of Esso and I cooked up the Seuss Navy.

Starting small at one of the New York motorboat shows, we printed up a few diplomas, and we took about 15 prominent people into membership—Vincent Astor and sailors like that, who had tremendous yachts—so we could photograph them at the boat show receiving their certificates.

We waited to see what would happen. Well, Astor and Guy Lombardo and a few other celebrities hung those things in their yachts. And very soon everyone who had a putt-putt wanted to join the Seuss Navy.

The next year we started giving annual banquets at the Biltmore. It was cheaper to give a party for a few thousand people, furnishing all the booze, then it was to advertise.

And it was successful because we never mentioned the product at all. Reporters would cover the party and *they* would write our commercials for us. So, we would end up with national coverage about "The Seuss Navy met . . . ," and then they would have to explain it by talking about Esso Marine.

At the time war was declared, in 1941, we had the biggest navy in the world. We commissioned the whole Standard Oil fleet, and we also had, for example, the *Queen Mary* and most of the ships of the U.S. lines.

Then, an interesting thing happened. I left to join the Army. And somebody said, "Thank God Geisel's gone, he was wasting a great opportunity. He wasn't *selling* the product. We have Seuss Navy hats and we have Seuss

> Navy glasses and Seuss navy flags." He said, "These things should carry advertising on them."
>
> They put advertising on them, and the Navy promptly died. The fun had gone out of it and the Seuss Navy sank.[19]

For the Seuss Navy, Geisel had even designed a Naval flag. It showed the skeleton of a red herring in profile, wearing an admiral's hat, with a vague Mona Lisa smile on its face.[20]

In May, 1934, he was interviewed for the first time, by a reporter from Dartmouth College.

> You want an interview, a sort of life story, as
> it were, he asked the reporter.
> The student nodded.
> Truth or fiction?

Geisel proceed to explain:

> I just came back from Peru. . . . (where I) looked into the llama situation. . . . They can spit at you and aim every shot they make. . . . The biggest disappointment I ever had . . . was when I went to Dalmatia to study the Dalmatian dog situation. . . . I got there and found all the Dalmatian dogs were in England . . . I go all over looking for peculiar animals (and) I've discovered that God has turned out even more ridiculous creatures than I have.[21]

The interview proved three universal truths about Seuss:

* He always embellished (with a twinkle in his eye) the story of his life and books. He became particularly wary of questions that began "how you develop your (book) ideas?" That invariably launched him into a widely fanciful Seussian tale of strange lands with unpronounceable names, where he visited to get ideas;

* He and his wife Helen *were* world travelers (they visited Peru twice in two years—and after nine years of marriage, they had visited thirty countries[22]) and he did, indeed, get story ideas in wild locales: *The Lorax* (1971) was developed and written completely during a visit to Kenya (with his second wife Audrey);

* God did, indeed, create even more fanciful creatures than Seuss did.

Much later, science writer Chet Raymo compared the World of Seuss to the World of Nature, in an article "Dr. Seuss and Dr. Einstein: Children's Books and Scientific Imagination":

> A few years ago, when an insect called the thrips—singular and plural—was in the news for defoliating sugar maples in New England, I noted in my Boston *Globe* science column that thrips are very strange beasts. Some species of thrips give birth to live young, some lay eggs and at least one species of switch-hitting thrips has it both ways. Not even the wildest product of Dr. Seuss's imagination, I said—the Moth-Watching Sneth, for example, a bird that's so big it scares people to death, or the Grickily Gractus,[23] a bird that lays eggs on a cactus—is stranger than creatures, such as thrips, that actually exist.
>
> What about the Moth-Watching Sneth? Well, the extinct elephant bird of Madagascar stood eight feet tall and weighed a thousand pounds. In its heyday—only a century or so ago—the elephant bird, or Aepyornis, probably scared many a Madagascan half to death.
>
> Pick any Seussian invention and nature will equal it. Dr. Seuss's *McElligot's Pool* (Random) there's a fish with a kangaroo pouch. Could there be such a fish in the real world? Not a fish, maybe, but in South America there is an animal called the Yapok—a wonderfully Seussian name—that takes its young for a swim, in a waterproof pouch.[24]

Before Geisel got completely complacent, serendipity again played a large part in his life.

In the summer of 1936, the Geisels sailed for Europe aboard the M. S. Kungsholm. They visited the Alps; Geisel saw intrepid Alp animals clinging to sheer Alp mountain outcroppings. They traveled to Germany and saw the chill of the oncoming Nazi tide. Geisel was then thirty-two years old and the storm clouds of European politics left him saddened.

They returned on the same ship—the Kungsholm. And Geisel found himself caught in the drone of the engine.

Da-da-*Da*, Da-Da-*DUM*, Dum-De-*Da*, De-De-*Da*—there was some variation, but the rhythm stayed in his head. A lesser man would have turned to the nearest ship's bar and taken a drink, or two, or three to take the noise out of his head.

Seuss listened.

He couldn't shake the engine's rhythm. He found himself forming rhymes to the drone of the engine. He was on the Kungsholm for eight days on his return passage. Eight days of listening to the SAME engine rhythm. Eight days of rhyme schemes in his head.

The drone of the Kungsholm's engine became the driving energy of Dr. Seuss's career. It was as simple as that.

Da-da-*Da*, Da-Da-*DUM*, Dum-De-*Da*, De-De-*Da*.

Geisel may not have known what he was hearing, but the rhythm was forceful, hypnotic. Once captured by it, he was hooked. The rhythm didn't leave his head.

He didn't know what he was hearing, but there was a name to it. He may have heard the name at Dartmouth, or at Oxford. If he did, he probably forgot it.

He was hearing the rhythm of:

"'Twas the night before Christmas . . ." or . . .

"He flys through the air with the greatest of ease . . ."

He was hearing *anapestic tetrameter* (or something very much like it), which dates as far back as the ancient Greeks, who used it as a marching beat.

Geisel began hearing. . . . *And to Think That I Saw It on Mulberry Street*, surely the Mulberry street of his hometown of Springfield.

And he remembered:

> I was on a long, stormy crossing of the Atlantic, and it was too rough to go out on deck. Everybody in the ship just sat in the bar for a week, listening to the engines turn over: da-da-ta-ta, da-da-ta-ta, da-dat-ta-ta . . .
>
> To keep from going nuts, I began reciting silly words to the rhythm of the engines. Out of nowhere, I found myself saying, "And that is a story no one can beat; and to think that I saw it on Mulberry Street."
>
> When I finally got off the ship, this refrain kept going through my head. I couldn't shake it. To therapeutize myself I added more words in the same rhythm.[25]

The story began with a horse and wagon. Geisel made a list:

> A stupid horse and wagon
> Horse and chariot
> Chariot pulled by flying cat
> Flying cat pulling Viking ship
> Viking ship sailing up volcano
> Volcano blowing hearts, diamonds and clubs
>
> I saw a giant eight miles tall
> Who took the cards, 52 in all
> And played a game of solitaire. . . .[26]

It did not come easy—Geisel had to marry words with the rhythm (and he probably still didn't know what it was). What he perhaps knew instinctively, but did not, or could not, verbalize was: *the rhythm dictated the story; and the rhythm galloped.*

Without knowing why it worked, he may have sensed it was a perfect rhythm for a children's story.

* * *

There must be something about oceanliners. Compare Theodor Geisel's experience to an earlier experience of John Philip Sousa, returning from Europe: "In November, 1896, Sousa and his wife were conducting a vacation in Europe when he received a cable telling him that his band manager had died in New York City. Suddenly the many responsibilities of arranging his next tour fell on Sousa's shoulders. He booked passage for home immediately.

"As the ship began its voyage across the Atlantic, Sousa paced restlessly on the deck, absorbed in the many details and decisions awaiting him once he reached the United States. Suddenly, as he described it, 'I began to sense the rhythmic beat of a band playing within my brain.'

"The music didn't stop but continued for the entire voyage, playing the same themes and distinct melody over and over again. Although he didn't write down a note of the music while on board the ship, the moment Sousa reached shore he wrote it just as he heard it in his mind during the voyage. Not one note of the composition has been changed since that day," Elizabeth Van Steenwyk wrote in "It's a Sousapalooza," in the *A & E Monthly* magazine for July 1996 (Now *Biography* magazine). The composition Sousa heard in his head? "The Stars and Stripes Forever," named by President Reagan in 1987 as the official march of the United States. Van Steenwyk writes that a fragment of the musical store of "The Stars and Stripes Forever" is engraved on Sousa's tombstone.

* * *

He added picture after picture. And, fortunately kept the rhythm scheme. It took him six months before he was happy with the final manuscript. The working title was *A Story That No One Can Beat.*

And here the Geisel story turns into legend.

He took it into New York and showed it to children's book publishers. One, two, three turned it down, four, five—more. And more. And more turned it down. Much later, newspaper and magazine articles set the number from "the twenties" to as many as "into the forties"—the number of publishers who said no. And they said no simply because there had never been a story like his. The rhythm, the Seussian pictures as a children's book.

(We wonder how many book publishers recognized the rhyme scheme as anapestic tetrameter . . .)

And this is a story no one can beat, and to think that I saw it on Mulberry Street. . . .

Rejection after rejection, time after time.

It was too different; it wasn't wholesome enough; it didn't teach the right moral lesson; it wasn't right for children.

Geisel was in Manhattan one day, with the manuscript under his arm. It had been rejected twenty-seven times. *Twenty-seven times!*

And on the sidewalk he met Marshall McClintock, who had been at Dartmouth, one year behind Geisel.

"How are you Ted? And what do you have under your arm?"

Twenty-seven rejections . . .

"It's a book manuscript. A book for children. And I can't do anything with it. . . ."

Serendipity was with Geisel that day. They were standing outside McClintock's office building and he had just been named a children's book editor with The Vanguard Press.

McClintock, Geisel and the manuscript went into McClintock's office. . . . and met James Henle, president of The Vanguard Press and Evelyn Shrifte, staff editor.

And this is a story no one can beat . . .

. . . became literally true. Vanguard Press took the book that day, and only asked for a better title, which became . . .

And to Think That I Saw It on Mulberry Street.

And the little boy who was the hero of the story was renamed after McClintock's son, Marco. And the book dedicated to McClintock's wife, Helene.[27]

If . . . the wife of the McCann-Eriksson executive had been in her usual hairdresser's, she might not have seen *Judge* magazine with Geisel's Flit cartoon and would have never talked her husband into hiring Geisel to draw Flit cartoons . . .

If . . . Geisel had taken a different steamship to and from Europe, he may never have heard such the hypnotic drone that stayed in his mind hour after hour, day after day, until he began to answer it in rhyme. . . .

If . . . Geisel had been five minutes earlier or five minutes later, or even on the opposite side of the street, he might not have met Marshall McClintock and might have abandoned *A Story No One Can Beat* forever. The rhythmic drone of the Kungsholm's engine might just have faded from his inner ear.

Serendipity had again perched on Geisel's shoulder. Can we guess what it looked like? Perhaps it looked something like a Who from Whoville . . .

Marco first sees, on Mulberry Street the "stupid horse and wagon" Geisel jotted down during the Kungsholm voyage.

But the horse turns into a Zebra (on one page); the wagon turns into a chariot (on the next page); the zebra turns into a huge reindeer; the wagon turns into an Eskimo sled; the Reindeer turns into a Blue elephant topped by a Rajah on a covered throne; the sled become a four-wheeled circus wagon, complete with circus band (page after page of changes); a small sled on wheels is pulled behind the wagon and two giraffes help the elephant pull.

The whole parade comes to the corner of Mulberry Street and Bliss Street and needs an escort of motorcycle police. They pass the Mayor and Aldermen on a reviewing stand; a passing airplane drops confetti . . . The parade includes . . .

A Chinese man with chopsticks . . .
A magician doing tricks . . . and . . .
A man with a ten-foot white beard . . .

I swung 'round the corner
and dashed through the gate,
I ran up the steps
And I felt simply GREAT!

FOR I HAD A STORY THAT NO ONE COULD BEAT!
AND TO THINK THAT I SAW IT ON MULBERRY STREET!

Dr. Seuss married text, rhyme and art perfectly.

Here Seuss begins techniques which he uses in almost—almost—all Dr. Seuss books. You could think of it as *escalating sequences* or *escalating action.* The rhyme gallops—the pictures move from left to right, toward the next page and the action builds. Every page—text and pictures—contributes to a bigger—and better—next page. It is no wonder that one of the best critical reviews of a Dr. Seuss book was by a child who simply said:

"Whew!"

Children can read the lines; they can sing the lines; they can *SHOUT!* the lines; they can dance to the lines. And with the emphasis at the end of each page (and on the right side of each page), they are drawn to the next page.

And finally the action climaxes. The child says "Whew!" And often, the reader is back at the beginning.

As children's literature expert Selma G. Lanes wrote much later:

> Seuss cannily manages to magnify and multiply the sense of suspense in his stories, not so much by the ingenuity of his plots as by a clever and relentless piling on of gratuitous anxiety until the child is fairly ready to cry "uncle" and settle for any resolution, however mundane, that will

> end his at once marvelous, exquisite and finally, unbearable tension. The process is not unlike the blowing up of a balloon: bigger, bigger, bigger and finally, when the bursting point is reached, Seuss simply releases his grip and all tension, like trapped air, is freed.[28]

Mulberry Street appears so remarkably easy: he had the rhyme from the engine drone; he had some characters from his shipboard notes. It only took six months to write. Only six months. It was clearly not that easy. He later said:

> It's hard. I'm a bleeder and I sweat at it. As I've said before: The "creative process" consists for me of two things—time and sweat. And I've also said that too many writers have only contempt and condescension for children, which is why they give them degrading corn about bunnies. The difficult thing about writing in verse for kids is that you can write yourself into a box: If you can't get a proper rhyme for a quatrain, you not only have to throw that quatrain out but you also have to unravel the sock way back, probably ten pages or so . . . You find that you're not driving the car, your characters are driving it. And you also have to remember that in a children's book a paragraph is like a chapter in an adult book, and a sentence is like a paragraph.[29]

The Vanguard Press advertised the book with a line which would become remarkably accurate over the years:

> Booksellers, hitch on! This is the start of a parade that will take you places![30]

Authors often suffer post partum depression when a book is out and reviews are either nonexistent or fewer than they may have anticipated.

Mulberry Street generated a few reviews, but they were very favorable. And they managed to match the book. The best was the shortest: writing in *The New Yorker*, Nov. 6, 1937, Clifton Fadiman said:

> They say it's for children, but better get a copy for yourself and marvel at the good Dr. Seuss' improbable pictures and the moral tale of the little boy who exaggerated not wisely but too well.[31]

The New York Times wrote:

> Highly original and entertaining, Dr. Seuss' picture book partakes of the better qualities of those peculiarly American institutions, the funny papers and the tall tale. It is a masterly interpretation of the mind of a child in the act of creating one of those stories with which children often amuse themselves and bolster up their self-respect.[32]

Anne Carroll Moore, children's book expert for the New York Public Library reviewed *Mulberry Street* in *The Atlantic Monthly*. She wrote:

> So completely spontaneous that the American child can take it in his heart on sight . . . As original in conception, as spontaneous in the rendering as it is true to the imagination of a small boy.[33]

(Moore wanted him to speak at the New York Public Library, but at the right time, he could get no further than outside the front doors, he was so consumed with stage fright.)[34]

How as it that Geisel, as Dr. Seuss, could remain "true to the imagination of a small boy?"

Helen Palmer Geisel, from the perspective of a loving spouse, later said, "his mind has never grown up."[35]

By the late 1930s, Geisel had developed a whole vast universe of Seussian animals, made of clay, pipe cleaners, odds and ends . . . a vast Noah's Ark of curious creatures great and small, all generated from his imagination, including: "red turtles, purple elephants, and green camels with bizarre beaks and horns."[36] He made one particularly enchanting bearded creature's face by simply using an old-fashioned men's shaving brush.

They were, of course, his creative *workshop*, his *dream works*, to use the name of Steven Spielberg's production company. Did they speak to him and he to them? Figuratively, they spoke louder than words; they spoke in volumes to him. And he gave them voices and personalities in book after book. . . .

And there were his hats. He had a collection of hats from all over the world, including "a fireman's hat from Equator and a hat from a Czech functionary."[37] Hats and hats and hats.

And once, when Geisel was on a commuter train, from New York into New England, he saw a staid businessman sitting ahead of him, wearing a hat on the train.

And the Seuss in him asked: *What would happen if I knocked that hat off his head?* And the answer clearly was: *another would appear. And another. And another. And another.*

And his second book became *The 500 Hats of Bartholomew Cubbins* (1938). Instead of rhyme, Seuss wrote it in prose, but he didn't forget the rhyme scheme from *Mulberry Street*, he just put it aside for a while.

Young Bartholomew Cubbins, who wore a very small and drab red hat, and who lived in the Kingdom of Didd, happened to be on his way into town when the King passed by with his royal entourage. All citizens of Didd were required to remove their hats when the King passed by.

But when Bartholomew took off his hat, another appeared. And when he took that hat off, another appeared. And another, and another. Taken to the royal castle, the king's advisors, the wise men first then the oldest and *very* wisest men, couldn't figure out why hats kept appearing on Bartholomew Cubbins' head.

They kept track, one by one, then more and more; the Grand Duke Wilfred, as young as Bartholomew, couldn't shoot one off with his bow and arrows, without another appearing instantly. The King's best archer, the "Yeoman of the Bowmen" also failed.

Seven royal magicians, each with a lean black cat, attempted to cast a spell, but the king wouldn't wait.

More hats appeared, a hundred and more . . . two hundred and more!

Bartholomew was ordered to the Royal Executioner to have his head cut off . . . but the Executioner wouldn't cut off anyone's head wearing a heat, so Bartholomew was spared.

And so Grand Duke Wilfred offered to pitch young Bartholomew off the highest turret in the castle. And up the winding stairs they went. But on the way, the hats began to change; they grew grander and grander . . . at the top of the tallest turret in the castle, Bartholomew stood, with the 500th hat, a grand, great hat on his head, a turban with jewels and feathers.

The King gave the Grand Duke Wilfrid a royal spanking for talking back to a King; and Bartholomew received 500 pieces of gold for his 500th hat.

> But neither Bartholomew Cubbins, nor King Derwin himself, not anyone else in the Kingdom of Didd could ever explain how the strange thing had happened. They could only say it just "happened to happen" and was not very likely to happen again.

Instead of the rhyme of the Kungsholm, *500 Hats . . .* was in prose; and instead of being completely in color, like *Mulberry Street . . .* it was in black and white; only Bartholomew's hats were in color, a bright, bright red. And unlike *Mulberry Street . . .* which was a contemporary children's story, *500 Hats . . .* was clearly a classic fable.

It also received favorable reviews, including *The New York*

Times and *Book List* and about the same number as *Mulberry Street*. . . .

A fellow member of the Dartmouth *Jack-o-Lantern* with Seuss, Alexander Laing was the most perceptive:

> That he is a rare and loopy genius has been common knowledge from an early epoch of his undergrad troubles. It now becomes plain that his is the self-consistent, happy madness beloved by children. I do not see what is to prevent him from becoming the Grimm of our times.[38]

Another serendipitous event approached; Geisel got a call from Bennett Cerf.

Cerf, a native of New York, had attended Columbia University's School of Journalism (when it was an undergraduate school—it later became solely a graduate program). Cerf had inherited $125,000 from a grandmother and decided after Columbia, to be a stockbroker. It wasn't right for him nor he for it.

So, in 1923, Cerf joined Horace Liveright in his firm Boni & Liveright. And for a contribution of $25,000 from Cerf, Liveright immediately made him a Vice President. Boni & Liveright was a quick education for Cerf; Liveright had a number of name authors, including Theodor Dreiser. But Liveright was a born gambler; profits he made by accident through Boni & Liveright were eaten up financing Broadway plays.

Eventually Cerf had to invest another $25,000 to help keep Boni & Liveright afloat.

In 1925, two years after he joined Boni & Liveright, Cerf offered to buy The Modern Library. In a financial bind (Liveright operated in no other way), he sold The Modern Library to Cerf for $200,000 (plus an "adviser fee" which Liveright tacked onto the deal at the last moment). Cerf brought in, as partner, Donald Klopfer, to join him, for $100,000. Klopfer, who came from a wealthy family, had no trouble finding $100,000 to join Cerf. The Modern Library had been sitting idle, making Horace

Liveright virtually nothing; two years after Cerf and Klopfer bought it, they had recouped their entire investment, including the additional $15,000 adviser's fee which they had to play Liveright.[39]

By 1926, Cerf and Klopfer decided to publish other books which they couldn't fit in The Modern Library series. In his autobiography, Cerf writes:

> Rockwell Kent had become a great friend of ours after he did the end papers for The Modern Library. I would say he was at that time the leading commercial artist in America. One day Rockwell dropped in at our office. He was sitting at my desk facing Donald, and we were talking about doing a few books on the side, when suddenly I got an inspiration and said, "I've got the name of our publishing house. We just said we were going to publish a few books on the side at random. Let's call it Random House."
>
> Donald liked it, and Rockwell Kent said, "That's a great name. I'll draw your trademark." So sitting at my desk, he took out a piece of paper and in a few minutes drew Random House, which has been our colophon ever since."[40]

The Random House house, in all its variations over the years, has become one of the most recognizable colophons in the country, matched by few others—the Viking Press Viking ship; the Henry Holt owl; the Alfred Knopf borzoi; the Bantam Books rooster and the Pocket Books kangaroo.

Random House made its reputation in the publishing world in 1934, when Cerf and Klopfer successfully published James Joyce's *Ulysses* in the United States when no other publisher would carry the obvious obscenity case through the U.S. Courts. When Judge John M. Woolsey ruled that *Ulysses* was "a sincere and serious attempt to devise a new literary method for the observation and description of mankind":

> We published *Ulysses* in January, 1934, with Woolsey's landmark decision in it—and it is still included in our edition. The book has had an enormous sale; it is one of the leading Modern Library and Vintage Giants and sells thousands of copies every year.

Cerf wrote.[41]

Random House expanded rapidly. Cerf brought in Eugene O'Neill and Robinson Jeffers, published the first American edition of Marcel Proust's *Remembrance of Things Past,* Gertrude Stein's *The Geographical History of America or The Relation of Human Nature to the Human Mind* (with dust jacket copy written by Cerf saying he didn't understand a thing she had written, but was publishing it anyhow.[42]). Cerf's coterie of known authors brought in more known authors: he added W. H. Auden and Stephen Spender, Havelock Ellis, George Bernard Shaw, William Saroyan, Budd Schulberg . . . Irwin Shaw, and others.

In 1936, Cerf offered to buy a fledging firm, Smith and Hass, which was having a hard time becoming established and staying financially solvent, bringing along founder Robert Hass as partner.

Hass accepted Cerf's offer and immediately Random House included William Faulkner, Andre Malraux, Robert Graves, Edgar Snow . . . and others.

Busy with adult titles and the growth of the firm, Cerf failed to notice that children's books could and should be emphasized in Random. His wife nudged him in the right direction:

> It was Phyllis who was . . . responsible for my thinking seriously about the books we published for children. She felt we were not doing the kinds of books that could

> help our own children expand the knowledge they were gaining in school.
>
> The first juvenile book I personally signed for Random House was by the now famous Dr. Seuss—Theodor Geisel. He had written two juveniles for Vanguard Press, but the one he did for us in 1939 was *The Seven Lady Godivas.*[43]

Cerf brought Geisel into Random House not knowing exactly what Geisel wanted to do next.

The Seven Lady Godivas was intended to be an adult retelling of the Lady Godiva saga, with typical Seussian twists. It begins:

> Forward. History has treated no one so shabbily as it has the name of Godiva. Today Lady Godiva brings to mind a shameful picture—a big blonde nude trotting around town on a horse. In the background of this picture, there is always Peeping Tom, an illicit snooper with questionable intentions. The author feels that the time has come to speak: *There was not one; there were Seven Lady Godivas, and their nakedness actually was not a thing of shame.*

The stories of each of the seven Godiva sisters (Teenie, Dorcas, Arabella, Mitzi, Lulu, Gussie and Hedwig) illustrates a variation of Horse Truths. And, for Seuss enthusiasts who have never seen a copy of *Godivas* . . .

Father Lord Godiva decides to go to the Battle of Hastings in 1066 on horseback. There are so much good-byes and cheering by the seven Godiva sisters that his horse Nathan reared, throwing him . . . and Lord Godiva was killed.

Each sister swears an oath to bring forth a new Horse Truth: because "*So long as your page remains empty of Horse Truth, so shall your life remain empty of love . . .*

* Teenie inspects a horse in the castle's stables, which had been presented to her late father, Lord Godiva. Imprudently, she opened its mouth to check its teeth . . . and the horse bit off her nose.

Horse truth: *never look a gift horse in the mouth.*

Teenie married Peeping Tom.

* Dorcas invented a Wagon Superior, with the cart above the horse, but it didn't work; she then invented a Wagon Inferior, with a sled below the horse. It too, was failure—the horse had to walk bowlegged. She then invented a Wagon Anterior, with the cart in front of the horse. The cart crashed into a tree.

Horse truth: *never put a cart before a horse.*

Dorcas married Peeping Dick.

* Arabella worked her poor horse Brutus 'way, 'way too hard and the horse turned to a vat of fermented alcohol and got drunk. She tried to pull the horse away from the vat to water, but it refused.

Horse truth: *You can lead a horse to water, but you can't make it drink.*

She left a note for the other sisters: "By the time you Old Maids read this, I'll be Mrs. Peeping Harry."

* Mitzi built a boat (The Peeping Jack I) propelled by a horse on a treadmill but it wasn't powerful enough. She then built a second boat (the Peeping Jack II) with room enough for two horses, who could change places when one was tried. But one ran into the other and the boat capsized.

Moral: *never change horses in the middle of a stream.*

Mitzi married Peeping Jack at sea.

* Lulu got kicked in the hayloft by a horse and when she fell into a haystack, she found Peeping Drexel's diamond stick-pin.

Moral: *horseshoes are lucky.*

She married Peeping Drexel.

* Gussie thought and thought and could discover no Horse Truth of her own. Finally she went to the stable with a large package and when she emerged—she was riding a blue-green horse—proving, awkwardly, but a Horse Truth nonetheless . . .

It was a horse of a different color.

She married Peeping Sylvester.

* Hedwig's horse Parsifal came down with the grippe. She was afraid she would lose him, so she stayed in the barn and nursed him through. She finally collapsed and fell asleep—when she awoke, Parsifal was gone. Parsifal had been stolen. She left, disconsolate . . . but remembered to snap the lock closed as she left.

Moral: *don't lock the barn door after the horse is gone . . .*

She married Peeping Frelinghauysen.

The Seven Lady Godivas is a charming, charming book . . . written in prose, not in Seuss's rollicking rhyme scheme.

But it was an abject failure. "We charged two dollars for *The Seven Lady Godivas*. It was the Depression. Nobody had two dollars," Geisel later said.[44]

But that was only partly true. Since librarians had filed the previous two Seuss books in the juvenile section of local libraries, they assumed that *Godivas* . . . was also a children's book, but they wanted no part of the Godiva fable in any children's literature section, specially with illustrations—any kind of illustrations. There were nudes in the book—the Godiva sisters, but they were the typical lumpy, mis-shapen Seuss drawings; he couldn't draw breasts or knees. It wasn't erotic. The book wasn't prurient enough for adult readers.

It was every author's nightmare: a royalty statement for a six month period ending Dec. 31, 1940 showed:

9 copies sold with a ten percent royalty:	$1.57
14 copies sold at a discount price of 9.80	.98
Total royalty	$2.55

A previous accounting showed a debit balance of $103.43. Thus the debit balance in Seuss's account was $100.88. When he received this royalty, Seuss drew a naked Lady Godiva on the bottom right margin, riding on a discouraged, bedraggled donkey, holding a banner reading "Excelsior!" and returned it to Cerf.[45]

The Seven Lady Godivas was the lowest point in Dr. Seuss's publishing career, but neither he nor Cerf were particularly crushed. Cerf regarded the loss as the price of luring Geisel to Random House. (Geisel cajoled Cerf into re-issuing *Godivas* in a Commemorative Edition years later, but it too, was a failure.)

The "Excelsior!" flag was as much for Geisel as it was for Cerf. Prior to the publication of *Godivas* . . . Geisel had quit working for Standard Oil. He remembered the starving men in the streets during the Depression, with this ode:

> A flock of Obsks
> From down in Nobsks
>
> Hiked up to Bobsks
> To look for Jobsks.
>
> Then back to Nobsks
> With signs and Sobsks . . .
>
> There were, in Bobsks,
> No jobs for Obsks.[46]

Dr. Seuss didn't forget The Obsks. They eventually reappeared in *If I Ran the Zoo* . . .

As children's book critic Selma G. Lanes said later:

> It's hard to resist watching for what will spring next from the mind of a man who would feed an "obsk" a vegetarian diet of "corn on the cobsk."[47]

Bennett Cerf must have known that his gamble on Dr. Seuss would eventually pay off, quite literally for decades.[48]

Three

1939–1948

"I meant what I said and I said what I meant . . .
An elephant's faithful— one hundred percent!"

Undaunted by the failure of *The Seven Lady Godivas*, Geisel plunged into *The King's Stilts*, a fairy tale written in prose.

His notes show the development of the villain, Lord Droon:

> Even as a baby, (he) was a scowler . . . Had no use for a rattle . . . preferred to rub two pieces of slate together . . . He liked rasping noise . . . When they gave him blocks with the alphabet on them, he would only use three. He was always spelling BAH![1]

King Birtram ruled in the kingdom of Binn, which was surrounded on three sides by the sea. Mighty Dike Trees kept the sea from pouring in but a kind of a blackbird called Nizzards kept attempting to eat the Dike Trees. The only thing to keep the Nizzards from the Dike trees were the largest and smartest cats in the kingdom. They were the Patrol Cats, who wore badges labeled P.C.

The King worked and worked and his only pleasure was his

pair of bright red stilts. No one begrudged him his stilts except for one old man:

> But there was one man in Blinn who didn't like fun. He didn't like games. He didn't like laughing. This man was a scowler. This man was Lord Droon. "Laughing spoils the shape of the face," he declared. "The lines at the corners of the mouth should go *down*."[2]

So Lord Droon stole the King's stilts and gave them to the king's pageboy named Eric, and demanded Eric hide them. The King went into a funk; the Patrol Cats no longer patrolled to keep the Nizzards away from the Dike Trees and all became hopeless.

But eventually, pageboy Eric couldn't stand keeping the secret of the hidden stilts and he ran to tell the King where he had buried them.

But Lord Droon tricked Eric by making him believe he had the measles and quarantined him in an old house. Eric escaped from quarantine and only just in time discovered sea water which had begun to trickle through the Kingdom. He ran and got the stilts which he had buried and gave them to his King.

On his red stilts, the King commanded the Patrol Cats to attack the Nizzards. It was a terrible battle and beautiful to behold. The Patrol Cats chased away the Nizzards, the Dike Trees again saved the kingdom and . . . The king and Eric both played together on their matching sets of red stilts.

But *The King's Stilts* sold little better than *The Seven Lady Godivas*. In his autobiography, Bennett Cerf was the very soul of courtesy about his new author: "In that same year (1939) we published his *The King's Stilts*, a juvenile which didn't sell many copies either."[4] The first year of publication, *Stilts* sold 4,648 copies and the next year's sales were down to 394 additional copies sold.[5]

Serendipity waited and bided its time, to appear the next year in the shape of a slight breeze from outside his studio window. . . .

Geisel was in the habit of working, then taking a break, and returning to work. He sometimes left a window open in front of his desk. When he returned during the day of January 2, 1940, he discovered that one drawing, of an elephant, had been blown across a drawing of a tree. The elephant appeared to be sitting in the tree.

What would an elephant be doing in a tree? Geisel asked.

Hatching an egg, Dr. Seuss replied.

And so he was.

And that led to feverish work—covering months.

In October, 1939, he wrote to Louise Bonino, juvenile book editor at Random House:

> The new book is coming along with a rapidity that leaves me breathless. It is a beautiful thing. The funniest juvenile ever written. I mean, being written. Never before have I stood before myself and pointed so proudly, saying "Genius, you are." I feel certain it will sell over a million . . . (Lew) Miller will hang himself with joy to every lamp post in town . . . (Robert) Haas and Klopfer will buy Tahiti and Bali respectively. (Saxe) Commins will buy Russia. Cerf will buy Hollywood. Louise Bonino will buy a negligee covered with sequins and umlauts and fine Nizzard Maribou . . . P.S.: I like my new book.[6]

The Seven Lady Godivas and *The King's Stilts* were charming stories, but they were stories. They had conclusions, but no real moral. *And to Think That I Saw It on Mulberry Street* had a moral; the moral it taught children was that their imaginations were as real as Marco's—and occasionally they should (or must) shield their imaginations from adults.

With *Horton Hatches the Egg*, Geisel returned to the galloping, rollicking, anapestic tetrameter rhyme scheme of *And To Think That I Saw It on Mulberry Street.*

Geisel worked at the plot as hard as he worked on any plot. Horton was first named Osmere, then Bosco, then Humphrey.

Finally Geisel chose Horton, after a classmate at Dartmouth, Horton Conrad.

Through a rainstorm, (so the story begins) and through snow and sleet of winter he sat while all the other creatures of the forest laughed and laughed . . . at an elephant sitting on a nest, hatching the eggs of a bird named Mayzie.

Hunters came; they aimed rifles at Horton (and Dr. Seuss shows Horton defiantly sitting, his forelegs—arms—folded across his chest).

So the hunters caged Horton—and the egg and the tree—hauling him ("egg, nest and tree") over craggy mountains, across the ocean in a ship, where they sold him as a circus act.

But one day, when the circus was not so far from Palm Beach, a bird flew over the tent, then inside the tent. Horton turned white—it was Mayzie. And she wanted her egg back. But the egg hatched an elephant bird!

> They cheered and they *cheered* and they CHEERED more and more.
> "They'd never seen anything like it before!
> *"My goodness! My gracious!"* They shouted. "MY WORD!
> IT'S AN ELEPHANT-BIRD!!
>
> And it should be, it *should* be, it SHOULD BE like that!
> Because Horton was faithful! he sat and he sat!
> He meant what he said
> And he said what he meant. . . ."[8]

Bennett Cerf and everyone else at Random were pleased with the manuscript of *Horton* . . . when it arrived. Cerf was so pleased that when Geisel requested an additional advance from royalties of five hundred dollars to buy a place in La Jolla, Cerf immediately sent it. When *Horton* . . . was published, it was an immediate hit. There were several reasons why it was a hit when *The Seven Lady Godivas* and *500 Hats* . . . were not: Dr. Seuss had a hero, Horton, which children could identify with—Horton had made a promise and had trouble keeping it.

Horton . . . was the first Dr. Seuss book with the hero speaking in the first person "I"—which children could also repeat: "*I* meant what *I* said and *I* said what *I* meant . . ."; it had a moral that children could understand: *you must keep a promise* and Geisel had gone back to the galloping rhyme scheme of the anapestic tetrameter, instead of static prose. Children could sing, chant, *shout!* the words. And the marriage of pictures and text was again, perfect.

The *New York Times* reviewer said:

> A moral is a new thing to find in a Dr. Seuss book, but it doesn't interfere much with the hilarity with which he juggles an elephant up a tree. To an adult the tale seems a little less inevitable in its nonsense, but neither young nor old are going to quibble with the fantastic comedy of his pictures.[9]

Then the coming war interrupted Dr. Seuss.

Ted Geisel showed a cartoon he had drawn to a friend, Zinny Vanderlip Schoales, who in turn showed it to Ralph Ingersoll, who had been a Jesus (a managing editor; "Jesus" was a *New Yorker* corruption of "genius") on the staff of *The New Yorker* before establishing the liberal newspaper *PM.* Ingersoll liked what he saw and invited Geisel to become a staff cartoonist.

Liberal Geisel was perfect for liberal *PM.*

The fact that *PM took* no advertising made it a perfect Seussian adventure—that was only one step removed from *Judge*, which *got* no advertising. At least Geisel was paid by *PM*; he didn't have to try and live on due bills for rooms in Atlantic City hotels.

Geisel called Charles Lindberg "one of our nation's most irritating heroes," and in cartoon after cartoon, Dr. Seuss ridiculed Hitler, when others were only taking a wait-and-see attitude.

In June, 1941, Ted and Helen Geisel moved to California,

into a home in La Jolla Shores for the summer. The hillside lot and home cost them—in 1940 dollars—eight thousand dollars.

> All the enlightened members of this community know about my books . . . but nobody in Southern California keeps 'em in stock . . . I gotta go now and fight rattlesnakes, bees and man-eating rabbits in the patio, then go fight Lindberg.

he wrote book editor Evelyn Shriffe.[10]

When war was declared, Dr. Seuss entered the fight with surprisingly acidic cartoons. He showed Hitler and a pig-faced Japanese emperor on Mount Rushmore with the caption:

DON'T LET THEM CARVE THOSE FACES
ON OUR MOUNTAINS!
BUY UNITED STATES SAVINGS BONDS
AND STAMPS![11]

His figures, cartoons and icons were right on target: Australian was shown as a kangaroo, with its tail being eaten by the Japanese; Nazis were shown as dachshunds—at least until American dachshund owners complained.

Four months after war with Japan, Germany and Italy was declared by Franklin Roosevelt, Geisel learned that Senator Gerald Nye of North Dakota had still called for the U.S. to stay out of the war.

"He's a horse's ass," Geisel said.

"You shouldn't use language like that," his wife said.

"He is a horse's ass and I'll draw him that way," Geisel said.

And he did—in *PM*.

Helen warned him he could get into real trouble for printing a cartoon showing Nye as a horse's ass.

Ingerosoll printed the cartoon but warned Geisel that he could get into real trouble for printing a cartoon showing Nye as a horse's ass.

Then Nye wrote to Geisel: "Dear Dr. Seuss: Please I would love to acquire that charming picture you made of me for my rumpus room."

But did he really write that? Seuss embroidered the tale slightly. What Nye did write was: "(The) issue of Sunday, April 26th . . . carried a cartoon, the original of which I should like very much to possess. May I request its mailing to me?"

Geisel asked Helen if he should mail it.

"No," she said, "he's a horse's ass."[12]

The Geisels moved from New York to their La Jolla home. But before leaving, Theodor Geisel, at thirty-eight, was inducted into the Army as a Captain and assigned to the Information and Education Division, in Hollywood.

California had become threatened by supposedly imminent invasion by the Japanese; with their property in La Jolla, the Geisels found that the war had indeed, come to them. Helen Geisel wrote to Evelyn Shrifte, across the country:

> There isn't a maid or gardener to be hand. Literally everyone is working for Consolidated (Aircraft) unless he's in uniform. One house is right up in no-man's land. Once a week the marines invade, and usually capture our hillside. We are dive-bombed at 5:30 A.M.—then we look out of the window to see hundreds of little boats, amphibious tanks, etc., rushing to shore. In a few minutes our house is in the midst of it all—tanks, jeeps, trucks, bayonets bared right on the driveway. The din of black cartridges is so terrifying that I can't even conceive of what the real thing must be like![13]

Geisel joined his unit, which was quickly dubbed "Fort Fox," working under director Frank Capra. Working with Geisel were composer Meredith Willson, novelist Irving Wallace and producer Carl Foreman. Supervising civilians were animators Chuck Jones and Friz Freleng.

> "(Geisel) tried so earnestly in field drills that it was touching. He was warm and full of worthy convictions, and patriotic to the limit, but he was hopelessly uncoordinated. He was tall, skinny, his hair parted in the middle and falling like some of the birds he drew, and with that great beak of a nose. . . .

author Paul Horgan told Neil Morgan.[14]

For Geisel, Hollywood during the war was another kind of Dartmouth or Oxford; this time for adults, not youngsters. They bought a home in Hollywood and Geisel absorbed script writing techniques from Frank Capra and grew to have an intense and lasting friendship with animator Chuck Jones, he of Bugs Bunny fame.

Geisel was part of a training film team to teach G.I.s cleanliness, avoidance of VD and other military matters. Geisel and company learned that if they showed average spokesman in the films, the recruits wouldn't listen; if they used Hollywood actors, the G.I.'s jeered at the screen. They *would* pay attention to cartoons, so Geisel and his troop created Private Snafu to explain things. Snafu was, of course Army slang for: *S*ituation *N*ormal *A*ll *F*—ked *U*p. They changed Snafu to: Situation normal ALL FOULED UP. The troops still loved it.

Geisel also worked on a film titled *Your Job in Germany*, which attempted to teach occupying troops never to fraternize with the defeated Nazis. Geisel wrote:

> The Nazi party may be gone, but Nazi thinking, Nazi training and Nazi trickery remains. The German lust for conquest is not dead . . . You will not argue with them. You will not be friendly. . . . There must be no fraternization with any of the German people.[15]

But Geisel couldn't escape his German-American heritage and he wrote the script half-heartedly, at best.

He was able, however, to tour Europe behind the Allied armies, carrying his film to show to troop units. He flew to Ireland, then England, then France and then throughout the Allied theater. Geisel found Generals Omar Bradley and Frank McSherry who approved the film for their troops. Only General George Patton refused. Geisel didn't have the opportunity to show it to Patton; someone else did and the General's sole comment was "Bullshit."

After Patton's resounding veto, Geisel traveled to a quiet sector of the war for some sightseeing, only to narrowly miss being taken prisoner by the Germans as the Battle of the Bulge erupted in the same area only hours later.

Back in Hollywood, Geisel's next assignment was to warn of a potential World War Three. He had read in *The New York Times* that a bomb could be built with huge destructive power, from only a glass of water, if only the energy in the water could be harnessed for a bomb.

The script made its way up the chain of a command—then Geisel got a call. The script contained vital secrets—Geisel was to burn the source of his information.

"Burn *The New York Times?*" he asked.

"Burn it," the anonymous voice said.

So Geisel found a copy of the *Times*—any copy—and burned it in a wastebasket in front of witnesses. Mission accomplished.[16]

The war ended soon enough, and Geisel survived it, but tragedy struck from another quarter; the Japanese surrendered in August, 1945, but in September, Geisel learned that his youngest sister Marnie had died. He had delayed his marriage for the birth of her baby and now she was dead. Her marriage had gone sour; she had moved back to the Geisel family home, but had become an alcoholic. She died at the age of forty-three, of a coronary thrombosis.

True to his stoic German heritage, Theodor Geisel never spoke of her death—ever.

After the war, Geisel stayed in Hollywood. Warner Brothers had heard about *Your Job in Germany* and had doctored it enough to win an Academy Award for their version, titled *Hitler Lives?*

Warner Brothers hired him and assigned him to director Jerry Wald. Wald assigned him to work on the script for the James Dean vehicle, *Rebel Without a Cause*. Geisel found it impossibly frustrating. The only element of a script he produced which was acceptable was the same title. Wald and Warners took everything else out.

He was then assigned to RKO, who wanted him to write a Japanese version, to be titled *Your Job in Japan*. Geisel hired Helen and the two of them began scripting the film. In one sequence, they had pastoral shots of sixteenth-century Japan. They were more than astonished when they ran the sequence and discovered someone had spliced in shots of American Sherman tanks. The tanks were edited back out.

> RKO called the documentary *Design for Death*; it went through thirty-two major revisions to eventually become a forty-eight minute film, with forty-five hundred feet of captured Japanese film spliced in.[17]

It won an Academy Award, the second Geisel had been involved with in two years. Neither of the films survive; they were probably withdrawn by the military and eventually lost of destroyed.

Geisel then got a call from a friend, offering them a vacation retreat in Palos Verdes Estates, near Los Angeles. The Geisels accepted immediately and moved in. The house—rather the estate, for it was built like a villa from the Italian Renaissance—had, as they say, a storied past. Myrna Loy had lived there, with Arthur Hornblower; Paulette Goddard and Burgess Meredith had honeymooned there.

After only a few days, Geisel decided that he wanted to live in a climate where he could "walk around outside in my pajamas."[18] So with the villa as a backdrop, and walking around outside in his pajamas when he pleased, Geisel began work on the first Dr. Seuss book in seven years.

He returned mentally and psychologically to his home town of Springfield and *And To Think That I Saw it on Mulberry Street* for his next book. There are striking similarities—and some differences—between *Mulberry Street . . .* and *McElligot's Pool.*

McElligot's Pool contains the same *escalating sequences* or *escalating action* that Geisel used in *Mulberry Street . . .* and the same hero—Marco. He is told that he won't catch anything fishing in McElligot's Pool, because it is full of junk.

But like Marco's parade on Mulberry Street, this time Marco imagines there is more in McElligot's Pool than boots, cans, tires and bottles.

The pool, Marco believes, winds its way under farm pastures and villages . . . and it might wind its way all the way down to the sea.

*   *   *

As a personal aside, *McElligot's Pool* was the first Dr. Seuss book that I remember reading, when I was about four, perhaps, going on five. I remember to this day following the pictures of McElligot's Pool winding its way underground to the sea thinking then: *it could happen just like that.*

Shortly thereafter, I was taken by my parents from our home in north central Ohio to The Blue Hole, a private park, which I remembered as being 35–40 miles from Lake Erie. I rechecked an Ohio map recently. In a straight line, The Blue Hole, in Castalia, Ohio, is about 8–10 miles from Lake Erie. I remember it as a brilliant crystal blue aquamarine spring. I couldn't see any fish. While we were there, a guide told us, "We don't know how, but we believe that The Blue Hole is connected underground to Lake Erie."

Just like Dr. Seuss said, I remember thinking.

Augmented by visiting The Blue Hole, my memory of reading *McElligot's Pool* for the first time never faded.

And that's duplicated, I am sure, by the millions of children who read a Dr. Seuss book for their first time and thought: *It could happen just like that! Just like Dr. Seuss said!* And I still have my copy of *McElligot's Pool.*

* * *

And Marco's line might find its way down to the sea.

(Dr. Seuss shows Marco's line with a worm wrapped around it in a loose knot, not hooked to it.)

Instead of merely thinking of catfish first, Dr. Seuss imagines a dog fish, chasing catfish.

Marco imagines fish swimming from the Tropics, and from north beyond Hudson's Bay, just to get caught in McElligot's Pool.

> A fish that's so big, if you know what I mean,
> That he makes a whale look like a tiny sardine!
>
> Oh, the sea is so full of a number of fish,
> If a fellow is patient, he *might* get his wish!
>
> And that's why I think
> That I'm not such a fool
> When I sit here and fish
> In McElligot's Pool.

And so *McElligot's Pool* ends very much like *And To Think That I Saw It on Mulberry Street . . .*

And where Dr. Seuss has a choice in illustrations—where slanting or movement is called for—the movement is invariably to the reader's right, pulling the young reader's attention toward the next page.

Geisel was so taken with the Italian vila atmosphere of his retreat in Palos Verdes Estates, that he painted all the illustrations in watercolor, a new technique for his books. But when the manuscript and illustrations reached Random House, production people there declared that the budget for the book only allowed half the color work he wanted. Few readers ever noticed that the first text page is in black-and-white, the next two in color, the next two in black-and-white and so on throughout the book.

McElligot's Pool won Dr. Seuss his first Caldecott award for the best children's book of the year and it was a selection of the Junior Literary Guild.

The dedication was to Geisel's Father—and the dedication was a family joke:

> This book is dedicated to
> T. R. Geisel of Springfield, Mass.,
> The World's Greatest Authority
> on Blackfish, Fiddler Crabs and Deegle Trout

Geisel had gone fishing once with his Father; but they had nothing to show for the excursion. So his father bought some trout at the Deegel Fish Hatchery and tried to pass them off as fresh-caught.[19]

Reviews continued to be very strong:

> This time prepare to chuckle under water for you'll be meeting the weirdest, wildest funniest creatures of the deep which imagination can conjure.
>
> —M.B. King, *Chicago Sun* Book Week[20]

> A picture book in rhyme, a book as divinely idiotic as the author-artist's And to Think That I Saw It On Mulberry Street, Grown-ups will have as much fun over

> the fish that the small fisherman MIGHT catch in McElligot's Pool as the children will.
>
> —S.J. Johnson, *Library Journal*[21]

> Children will have nothing but admiration for this boy who heard that there were no fish in McElligot's Pool and then saw them swimming in from the sea.
>
> —*Saturday Review of Literature*[22]

What morals can we draw from *McElligot's Pool?* First, be patient and things might happen. Secondly, trust your own instincts—don't believe what others tell you. Finally, and most importantly, there is a unity to all of nature. McElligot's Pool connects to the ocean; The Blue Hole connects to Lake Erie. To use the title of Holocaust survivor Elie Wiesel's memoir, *All Rivers Run to the Sea* (New York: Alfred Knopf, 1995).

Thereafter, Dr. Seuss books usually became an annual event.

The next year *Thidwick, The Big-Hearted Moose* made his appearance:

And so (the story begins) a Bingle-Bug hitched a ride on Thidwick's antlers—and then a Tree-spider joined, and began to spin a web on Thidwick's antlers, and then a Zinn-a-zu Bird who pulled hairs out of Thidwick's head.

But the next day Thidwick saw that the bird had been married and brought his wife, and uncle (who was a Woodpecker) along. The Woodpecker drilled four holes in Thidwick's horn.

A fox, some mice, some fleas, a big bear, and a swarm of three hundred and sixty-two bees came along. Hunters wanted to shoot him, for his antlers, to hang on the Harvard Club wall. So he ran, hunters in pursuit, up hills and down, with all his guests jouncing along. Onto a knoll, on the edge of the lake.

> *And finally his OLD horns came off so that NEW ones can grow!*

And he called to the pests on his horns as he threw 'em,
"You wanted my horns; now you're quite welcome to 'em!
Keep 'em! They're yours!
As for ME, I shall take
Myself to the far distant
Side of the lake!"

And he swam Winna-Bango and found his old bunch,
And arrived just in time for a wonderful lunch
At the south of the lake, where there's moose-moss
to munch.[23]

The reviewers chimed in:

> The author's rollicking verse is perfectly suited to this comical tale. His pictures in red, blue and black are expressive and funny, and though they appear slightly confusing at first glance, they are well adapted to the spirit of the story. For little children, it is splendid read-aloud nonsense.
>
> —*The New York Herald Tribune Weekly Book Review*[24]

> How Thidwick asserted himself is told in verses which march in double-quick time. The pictures are scenes of happy confusion, a little difficult to see at first, but as madly absurd as anything Dr. Seuss has done. This is pure entertainment for almost anyone over 5.
>
> —E. L. Buell, *The New York Times*[25]

> This popular author-artist has written another imaginative and hilarious tale which will be received with enthusiasm and delight by both adults and children. The pictures, which are in black, red and blue, are as comical as the text.
>
> —*San Francisco Chronicle*[26]

> The verses that tell this sad tale are very funny indeed, and the drawings of Thidwick are a delight, from the first page to the last.
>
> —M. G. Davis, *Saturday Review of Literature*[27]

An essay, "The Significance of Dr. Seuss," which captured the differences between Seuss and Disney and differences between how adults perceived the story and how children perceived the story, was written by David Dempsey in *The New York Times*:

> *Thidwick* is a masterpiece of economy, and a shrewd satire on the "easy mark" who lets the conventions of society get the better of him. The genius of the story, however, lies in its finale. A man of less consistence than Seuss would have let Thidwick be rescued by the creatures he is befriending (this is the customary Disney riposte in similar situations) but Seuss' logic is rooted in principle, rather than sentiment, and the sponging animals get what they deserve. Incidentally, this is also what the child expects.[28]

For his next book, Theodor Geisel drew on a fragment of conversation he overheard when he was in Europe during World War Two. On a rainy night in Belgium, trapped while the Battle of the Bulge raged nearby, Geisel overheard one G.I. say to another, "Rain, always rain. Why can't we have something different for a change?"[29]

And the voice of Dr. Seuss inside him asked, *"well, why can't we have something different for a change? Why is it always rain that falls from the sky?"*

And he again drew on Bartholomew Cubbins and the Kingdom of Didd. *Bartholomew and the Oobleck* was in prose, not in his rollicking anapestic tetrameter.

The King summoned his royal magicians to cast a spell to make something else came down from the sky, when he got tired of sun and rain and fog and snow.

And then Oobleck began to fall. First lightly, like snowflakes, then like rain, then like *very* heavy rain, then great goops of oobleck, *as big as cupcakes*, covering everything and everyone. Green, pea green oobleck, covering the bell in the bell tower so it couldn't chime; covering the royal trumpeter so he couldn't blow a warning; covering the Captain of the Guards, so he couldn't warn the people . . . and still it came down, as big as *greenish footballs*, covering the Royal Cook and the Royal Laundress and the Royal Fiddlers and—even the Royal King. And the oobleck kept falling, kept raining down on the Kingdom of Didd.

Bartholomew finally had to confront the King. To rid the Kingdom of Didd from the Oobleck would not involve magic spells or magic words—but only two simple words, Bartholomew told the King:

"Now, the least you can do is say the simple words, 'I'm sorry.'"

But then Bartholomew heard a great, deep sob. The old King was crying! "Come back Bartholomew Cubbins! You're right! It *is* all my fault! And I *am* sorry! Oh, Bartholomew, I'm awfully, *awfully* sorry!"

And the moment the King spoke those words, something happened . . .

Maybe there is something magic in those simple words, "I'm sorry."

The lesson was obvious for even the smaller reader—or listener—if the story was read to them:

Sometimes you have to say "I'm sorry."

Sometimes you have to say, "It's all my fault."

Even if you're a King.

Bartholomew and the Oobleck won Dr. Seuss his second Caldecott Award, for the best children's book of the year.

In the summer of 1949, Geisel was invited to speak at ten-day writers' conference at the University of Utah. Screwing up his courage to travel and speak to strangers, Geisel made the trip. He was in wonderful company: Vladimir Nabokov, who had come to the United States nine years earlier; western novelist Wallace Stegner, poets William Carlos Williams and John Crowe Ransom.

By that time, Geisel had strong, very strong beliefs about children's literature; those who write it and what made it exceptional. Children couldn't handle ancient myths, except those which were largely visual: Thor and his hammer, Hermes and his winged sandals.

Aesop's fables were too cold, the *Illiad* too complicated for the re-telling, but the *Odyssey* and the Robin Hood tales were adventurous. He also said he liked Hans Christian Andersen, Robert Louis Stevenson and Mark Twain.

Geisel suggested (can we see the twinkle in his eye?) where his place was: "in the realm of nonsense, there are Mother Goose, (Edward) Lear, (Lewis) Carroll, P.L. Travers and Dr. Seuss."[30]

And he analyzed the *logic* of the *insanity* of children's books:

> This is the crux . . . a man with two heads is not a story. It is a situation to be built upon logically. He must have two hats and two toothbrushes. Don't go wild with hair made of purple seaweed, or live fireflies for eyeballs . . . Children analyze fantasy. They know you're kidding them. There's got to be logic in the way you kid them. Their fun is pretending . . . making believe they believe it.[31]

Geisel assembled his lecture notes and suggested that Bennett Cerf and Random House publish a book of writing techniques for children's books authors. His proposal went first to the juvenile book editors at Random (probably the wrong place for it to land, for it would be a book for adults who were novice "kiddie lit" writers), then worked its way up the chain to Bennett Cerf . . .

. . . and came right back to Geisel.

Random House was *not* interested in such a proposal, for such a book.

Geisel was crushed. Perhaps even more so than when he collected twenty-seven rejections before Marshall McClintock and the Vanguard Press took *And To Think That I Saw It On Mulberry Street. . . .*

After all, then he was an unpublished writer; now he was an experienced author, with several books to his credit, Caldecott Awards and glowing reviews for his work. But the proposal was rejected nonetheless. Random editors didn't want him interrupting his usual work *to tell others how to do the same.*

Louise Bonino, juvenile editor, wrote the rejection letter Random House sent to Geisel:

> You enjoy the adulation not only of the general public but also of the children's librarians. . . . Some of them would feel an author-artist of picture books could hardly qualify as an expert in the field of juvenile writing. . . . (Saxe Commins's) concern is that it would interrupt you in the steady production of your marvelous children's books (and bring) down on your head all kinds of criticism for doing a semiformal book which tries to explain method when there is so much inspired madness in your own work . . . I am returning your notes under separate cover.[32]

Could hardly qualify as an expert in the field of juvenile writing. . . .

(We can only wonder now what he would have had to say in book length about the art of writing for children. And oh! what a missed opportunity for such a book from such a man . . . but the book publishing industry is full of such stories, of editors who make—or made—wrong decisions, refusing to allow an author such as Geisel work on a project the author wanted to work on. Or refusing to accept a book manuscript and thus losing a writer to another publishing firm. Bennett Cerf's own autobiography mentions other such cases. But in this case, we can suggest that Random House was truly wrong. What could it have cost them to allow Geisel to write the book he wanted to write?)

But Geisel moved on, figuratively and literally. Geisel's wife Helen had a family trust fund that had been accumulating interest over the years; they decided that they wanted to live someplace high. They turned to San Diego architect Tom Shepard who suggested an old observation tower on Mount Soledad that overlooked everything else in La Jolla, which they had first discovered some twenty years previously. They bought the tower and two acres around it immediately and sold their La Jolla Shores home and their Hollywood home.

And Geisel's purchase of the tower and the surrounding land was a joke on all of La Jolla. No one thought it was for sale; indeed, everyone living in La Jolla thought that it was government property, quite unavailable for sale.

In the past, servicemen had taken their dates there for quiet trysts; the view was spectacular and lovers' initials had been carved everywhere.

The Geisels could not only look over the city of La Jolla, but San Diego, sixty miles of shoreline of the Pacific and on clear days, they could see inland as far as Palm Springs and well into Mexico. They had a picnic on their new property in mid-September, 1948 and year or so later, they moved into their pink stucco home. And he brought his dinosaur footprint along.

For the rest of his life, he seldom left it for long. It would not surprise accomplished writers to learn that when he was concentrating, the vast views from "The Tower" escaped his attention; he literally turned his desk and his back to the view.

It was his aerie and Theodor Geisel was at home at the very top of La Jolla and in the vast high tower of his imagination.

Four

1948–1956

. . . he began to chart vast regions of his own, *the terra incognito of his Seussian world . . .*

Ted and Helen began to enjoy their new La Jolla home, in the spring of 1949, one year after the construction began. Getting accustomed to his new working quarters, his thoughts turned toward his childhood home in Springfield. And his bedroom, and the nights he heard the night sounds, the howls, the cries of the nearby Springfield Zoo. And he thought of his father, who took him to the Zoo; he remembered the trails, the animals, their names, their cages, their histories, the zoo smells, the workers, the visitors.

And he thought of the Kungsholm's engine drone, the anapestic tetrameter, which he had used so successfully in *And To Think That I Saw It on Mulberry Street . . .* , *Horton Hatches the Egg . . . McElligot's Pool* and *Thidwick the Big-Hearted Moose*, but abandoned in favor of prose in *The 500 Hats of Bartholomew Cubbins . . . The Seven Lady Godivas . . . The King's Stilts . . .* and *Bartholomew and the Oobleck.* He still heard the drone in his inner ear.

But most of all, he remembered a young boy.

And he thought . . .

And what? *And what?*

He liked to "approach a book with a solution or conflict and hen write myself into an impossible position so there is no (apparent) way of ending (the book). . . . people who think about the endings first come up with inferior products," he told biographers Judith and Neil Morgan.[1] Even if that meant "unraveling the sock" much further back in the earlier pages, if the rhyme scheme went off track or the plot didn't flow.

And what? He would fool with the characters on his desk, get up and walk, pace back and forth, smoke, toy with his *dream works*, until the situations and animals came. (And they came logically one step removed from reality, then a second-step removed from the first and then a third . . . until there was nothing in the world like Dr. Seuss creatures—except the little-known Seussian creatures in nature).

And not only *and what?* but *and where?* From the vast High Top tower overlooking the lush California fields and gardens, and the Pacific and Mexico that Theodor Geisel saw in the distance, he also saw a vast geography of locales . . . and places he knew intimately, because he had been there: Peru, Turkey, England, Italy, Europe.

And in *If I Ran the Zoo*, he began to chart vast regions of his own, the terra incognito of his Seussian world unknown to everyone else, but clearly and indelibly pictured to him. He began to chart the cartography of his mind. And there was no better place to begin than his La Jolla aerie, where he had a vast panorama in front of him, where his imagination could take him—as Gerald McGrew—over the horizon of the Pacific, as the first step to . . . the African Island of Yerka . . . the Mountains of Tobsk (near the River of Nobsk) . . . the jungles of Hippo-no-Hungus, Dippo-no-Dungus and Nippo-no-Dungus . . . the Island of Gwark . . . *and so forth and upward and onward, gee whiz!*

He remembered the Obsks, from his last days with Standard Oil, during the Depression, when he saw men selling apples on the streets of New York, bankrupt. And he even knew the Obsks' diet:

I'll go to the far-away Mountains of Tobsk
Near the River of Nobsk, and I'll bring back an Obsk,
A sort of a kind of a Thing-a-ma-Bobsk
Who only eats rhubarb and corn-on-the-cobsk.
Then people will flock to my zoo in a mobsk.
"McGrew," they will say, "does a wonderful jobsk!
He hunts with such vim and he hunts with such vigor,
His New Zoo, McGrew Zoo, gets bigger and bigger!"

If I Ran the Zoo is Theodor Geisel's clearest and most obvious acknowledgment of his own childhood. And in it, he began to take his readers to lands much richer and more fantastic than Mulberry Street and the Springfield Zoo. In doing so, his books became mirrors for the imaginations of his children-readers, reflecting their own worlds back to them—and validating in a way children could clearly understand, their own best-kept secrets—the worlds of their own imaginations: their own African islands of Yerka, their own Mountains of Tobsk (near the River of Nobsk), their own jungles of Hippo-no-Hungus, Island of Gwark and thousands of other enchanting and fantastical places and locales you and I have never dreamed of. . . .

Reviewers seemed to understand that Geisel had taken another step:

> (It) has a range and freedom of extravaganza that I found utterly delightful.
>
> —A.C. Moore, *The Horn Book* Magazine[2]

> As you turn the pages, the imaginings get wilder and funnier, the rhymes more hilarious. There will be no age limits for this book, because families will be forced to share re-reading and quotation, for a long, long time.

> Hurrah for you, Dr. Seuss, and thank you for one of the funniest children's books in a blue moon.
>
> —L. Bechtel, Books section, *The New York Herald Tribune*[3]

> Dr. Seuss has never imagined or created a better or funnier picture book than this one.
>
> —*The Saturday Review of Literature*[4]

> All the Dr. Seuss books are popular with children, as well as with the adults who read them aloud . . . This newest one is among the best.
>
> —Frances Chrystie, *The New York Times*[5]

While he was waiting for the book to appear from Random House, Geisel was approached by P. D. Eastman, whom he had known from the war years. Eastman and begun working for a new production company, United Productions of America, and they wanted something other than the typical (read Mickey Mouse) cartoons. Did Geisel have a story idea they could use?

He created a little boy, who didn't speak in words—he spoke only in sounds. He wrote a script and quickly received a check for five hundred dollars. UPA brought the story to life and Geisel watched as his story gained shape and form.

Gerald McBoing-Boing was almost a predecessor to Charles Schultz' Charlie Brown. Gerald has a round face with a blond topknot. He spoke only in sound effects, a crash! a bang! . . . He has no friends; everyone makes fun of him . . . and so he takes to the streets, an figurative orphan. But a talent scout spots him and he makes a fortune doing sound effects on the radio. His parents listen in the radio studio while he proves (for the first time) his success and at the end of the show, he and they ride off in a limousine.

It was, indeed, far, far different than the usual (Mickey) mouse-(Donald)duck-(Bugs)bunny cartoons of the day. *Gerald*

McBoing-Boing won an Academy Award for UPA in 1951. It was the third Academy Award project that Theodor Geisel had been involved with.

Theodor Geisel's next venture in Hollywood was completely the reversal of his earlier work—instead of everything going reasonably well, his next project went considerably awry.

The project was *The 5,000 Fingers of Dr. T*, a fantasy produced by Stanley Kramer. The Dr. T being Dr. Terwilliker, a name from his Springfield, Massachusetts youth. Bart (played by Tommy Rettig, of the television *Lassie* series), the hero of the story was (like Theodor years before, in Springfield) bored with his piano lessons. Falling asleep, he drifts (somewhat like Dorothy in the tornado swirling toward Oz) to the castle of Dr. Terwilliker (Hans Conreid), who rules over a piano keyboard two stories high, with 500 captive boys playing with all 5,000 fingers at the same time. Eventually Bart breaks the spell cast over the 500 reluctant piano players and Dr. T is defeated.

The Geisel left their Tower aerie in La Jolla, (which must have, itself, been a bad sign) and moved to Hollywood. There Geisel became the script writer, set designer, lyricist, unofficial producer and unofficial director and key cheerleader for the film.

The production was postponed, then postponed again. Geisel suffered agony after agony; the script was revised and revised again. The production was postponed—for the third time. Peter Lynd Hayes and Mary Healey were brought in as additional cast members. Geisel had to request Kramer delete some questionable scenes.

Eventually, the film went into production, but when Geisel counted heads, he found that the 500 young piano layers turned out to be 150.

Geisel's visualization of scenes involving 500 boy piano players was curtailed by the missing 350; his visualization of the plot, the set designs, and the logic of the story were crippled by the actual production. Nothing went as Geisel anticipated. He surely didn't anticipate that 350 of the 500 boy pianists would be AWOL; the 5,000 fingers of Dr. T eventually turned out to be the 1,500 fingers of Dr. T.

The project ended mercifully, with a epic Seussian accident: during a lunch break, all 150 boys were fed hot dogs from the studio commissary. One became ill and vomited on his own piano keyboard:

> That started a chain reaction, causing one after another of the boys to go queasy in the greatest mass upchuck in the history of Hollywood . . . when the picture was finally released, the critics reacted in much the same manner,

Geisel said.[6]

It was, for its time, a major investment. But there was no happiness and light on the set; rather, there was confusion, revisions, problems and boy after boy spewing hot dogs onto the set. The film eventually cost $2,750,000 to make; it was the most expensive film Stanley Kramer had made to that point. When it was previewed in Los Angeles, in January, 1953, patrons began walking out 15 minutes after the film began. By the end of the film, only five audience members were left, beside Geisel, Kramer and the crew.[8]

Even more than *The Seven Lady Godivas*, the disaster of *The 5,00 Fingers of Dr. T* caused Geisel permanent and devastating disappointment and embarrassment. After all, it was to be his supreme accomplishment in Hollywood. And he *had* been involved in three productions which had each won an Academy Award. In his mind, *The 5,000 Fingers of Dr. T* erased all his previous Hollywood accomplishments and added layer after layer of betrayal, distrust, anguish and embarrassment.

He retreated to his La Jolla tower, never ever to trust or believe in Hollywood again.

When he wasn't agonizing over the production of *Dr. T*, Geisel was working on another book for Bennett Cerf and Random House.

It came out after the production of *The 5,000 Fingers . . .* was over and it followed essentially the same plot as *If I Ran the Zoo*, and much of the same rhyme scheme. As much as Theodor Geisel had despaired of Hollywood during the production of *The 5,000 Fingers . . .* , Dr. Seuss remained right on track for his next book—*Scrambled Eggs Super!:*

(Dr. Seuss illustrates the first page with Peter T. Hooper talking to girlfriend Liz and the "when mother was out" will become a key element in other, later Dr. Seuss books—and with good reason: Dr. Seuss speaks to the hidden world of children: what happens to them when their parents are absent. He projects their own world on paper, in rhyme and pictures—he doesn't speak down to them from an adult's omnipotent point of view.)

The logic—and action—escalates just like *And To Think That I Saw It on Mulberry Street, McElligot's Pool* and *If I Ran the Zoo*.

In *Scrambled Eggs Super*, Dr. Seuss delivers even more colorful images than before: did Dr. Seuss make up creatures, like the "Grickily Gractus"?

Nature has given us a creature very much like the Grickily Gractus, writer Chet Raymo tells us ("Dr. Seuss and Dr. Einstein: Children's Books and Scientific Imagination," *The Horn Book* Magazine, September, 1992).

And his rhyme schemes get even more and more engaging and more and more convoluted and more and more fanciful (This is a Mobius loop of a poem):

> Then I went for some Ziffs. They're exactly like Zuffs,
> But the Ziffs live on cliffs and the Zuffs live on bluffs.
> And, seeing how bluffs are exactly like cliffs,
> It's mighty hard telling the Zuffs from the Ziffs.
> But I *know* that the egg that I got from the bluffs,
> If it wasn't a Ziff's from the cliffs, was a Zuff's.[9]

Eventually, Dr. Seuss brings all the bird-chasing and egg-hunting back to the kitchen (still without mother) makes a huge meal of eggs, beans, ginger, prunes, figs, parsley (quite sparsely) cinnamon sticks, and clove.

Scrambled Eggs Super received as much critical acclaim as other, previous Dr. Seuss books:

> When the one and only Dr. Seuss unleashes his famous imagination to run riot across the pages of a large-size picture book, hurrahs sound from every quarter. And so they will again at this wildly nonsensical account.
>
> —Polly Goodwin, *Chicago Sunday Tribune*[10]

> How one man can makeup such marvelous names and also draw pictures that surpass the names in fantastic imagery is a mystery. The "very best fowls" in this book are just as wild and funny as the animals in "If I Ran the Zoo." To an adult, the precise quality in the tall-tale style of young Peter T. Hooper adds to the fun of a hilarious creation.
>
> —L. Bechtel, Book Review section, *The New York Herald Tribune*[11]

> The bizarre names of the birds and the patter of the verse make this a wonderful book for reading aloud in the family. The pictures will amuse everyone.
>
> —*U.S. Quarterly Book Review*[12]

In March, 1953, Theodor and Helen Geisel sailed to Japan, to get the distaste of *The 5,000 Fingers . . .* out of their systems and to enjoy a long-delayed vacation. They received their first copies of *Scrambled Eggs Super!* as they were packing for the trip. On board the U.S.S. President Cleveland, sharing the voyage with them as far as Honolulu the Geisels were surprised to learn, were two former presidents, Herbert Hoover and Harry Truman. The bombings of Hiroshima and Nagasaki were only eight years previous and Geisel was eager to learn the extent of the changes (or the lack of changes) in Japan.

In Kyoto, Osaka and Kobe, Japanese schoolchildren had been invited to draw what they expected to be when the grew up: over 15,000 drawings had been submitted and Ted Geisel was somewhat shocked to see how "American" the drawings were. Boys wanted to fly or go to Mars, girls drew themselves as hostesses on busses. They returned on the U.S.S. President Wilson ("We only travel on ships named for Democrats," Geisel said) and he prepared an article about the Japanese children for *Life* magazine. The article, "Japan's Young Dreams"[13] was heavily edited by Henry Luce's staffers ("Henry Luce was always anti-Japanese and pro-Chinese and they raped the article," he said.)[14]

Most importantly, Geisel brought back trunkfuls of drawings by Japanese children.

The 5,000 Fingers of Dr. T was released about the time the Geisels returned from Japan. The reviews were as markedly bad as Geisel anticipated. Over the years, however, some lightness broke the darkness of that time. (After all, no one on the set at the time ever thought that *The Wizard of Oz* would be anything more than a quirky grade C+ film.) *The 5,000 Fingers of Dr. T* has become something of a cult classic—when and if it can be found. It is more highly regarded now than when it was made—but remains largely unavailable[15] (Although Columbia/TriStar released it on home video in 1991).

One day, in the spring of 1953, in New York, Geisel asked his literary agent, Phyllis Jackson if "I dropped everything else, do you think I could count on royalties of five thousand dollars a year?"[16] We can imagine his plaintiveness. But the question was serious. Geisel wanted nothing to do with Hollywood—where he knew he could make much, much more money—and he didn't want the distractions of writing for Luce's *Life* (or writing for *Life's* Luce). He did not yet anticipate (nor did anyone else) the enormous baby-boom generation, nor did he anticipate the eventual demand for Dr. Seuss books.

Every year, countless thousands of children "grow into" the readership level of Dr. Seuss books, just like growing into shoes. And then they would get Dr. Seuss books from their school or community library, take them home, color in them, lose them and the school or library would buy more Dr. Seuss books.

As of 1996, Dr. Seuss books have sold over 150,000,000[17] copies and, as much as we can be amused at Ted Geisel's 1953 question "do you think I could count on royalties of five thousand dollars a year?", it is a lesson for all writers. Eventually, you too, may—*may*—sell like Dr. Seuss. As the new century begins, he has set the benchmark for sales of children's literature. And just as certainly, the critical benchmark as well.

By the fall of 1953, Dr. Seuss again tackled a book, and this time strictly adhered to the rhyme scheme he used back as far as *And To Think That I Saw It on Mulberry Street . . .*

He tied together three key items: 1). The anapestic tetrameter he knew so well; 2). Horton, the elephant from *Horton Hatches the Egg* and a third element. . . .

The working title of the book was *Horton Hears 'Em!* but the 'Em (or them) eventually became Whos and the title was changed to *Horton Hears a Who!*:[18]

And when Geisel toured Japan he towered over his Japanese hosts. And he towered like a benevolent crane 'way, 'way over the heads of the Japanese children he met.

So he added a much more powerful moral then in any of the previous Dr. Seuss books. In *Bartholomew and the Oobleck*, the moral was:

> Sometimes you have to say:
> *I'm sorry. It's all my fault.*

But in *Horton Hears a Who!*, the moral was universal, multi-national, multi-ethnic. In a word: Equality. And it was especially meaningful for children, the way Dr. Seuss phrased it:

> I'll just have to save him. Because, after all,
> A person's a person, no matter how small.

(The voice of the Whos are set in type half the size of the Horton's, in much the same style as the Mouse's tale in *Alice in Wonderland*. His tale bends and twists down the page, set in increasingly smaller type. It is literally the Mouse's tale and his *tail*.)

But the Wickersham (another name from Ted Geisel's hometown of Springfield, Mass.) monkeys steal Horton's clover (with the Whos and Whoville) and give it to an eagle named Vlad Vlad-i-koff, who flew with it, Horton in pursuit all night.

Children would not know the metaphor Dr. Seuss uses, but if adults knew of his trip to Japan following World War Two, then the atomic bomb reference is clear:

> From down on the speck came the voice of the Mayor:
> "We've really had trouble! Much more than our share.
> When that black-bottomed birdie let go and we dropped,
> We landed so hard that our clocks have all stopped.
> Our tea-pots are broken. Our rocking-chairs smashed.
> And our bicycle tires all blew up when we crashed.

But the Kangaroos and the Wickersham monkeys and the Wickersham brothers and uncles and cousins all conspire to rope Horton and snare him. . . .

Horton told the Whos that they had to prove they were there—that each and every Who had to shout out loud that he or she was there. They shouted, but the Kangaroos and the Wickersham monkeys couldn't hear them. The kangaroos and the monkeys roped Horton and began pulling him into a cage. All the Whos in

Whoville still couldn't make themselves heard. The Whoville Mayor searched and he searched to make sure everyone was shouting, as loud as he could but nothing happened until the smallest Who shouted out the smallest shout.

Dr. Seuss phrased the moral two ways: The smallest voice can make a difference; and, a person's a person's no matter how small.

He also thought of McCarthyism, when U.S. citizens were afraid to speak their minds; when, he said they were "scared of speaking their thoughts aloud."[20]

After completing the manuscript and drawings for *Horton Hears A Who!* Ted and Helen Geisel relaxed in their La Jolla home; he was approaching his fiftieth birthday. There was some talk (and some work) on a Broadway production of *The Seven Lady Godivas*, but the project came to naught. He wrote the script for a half-hour television show, "Modern Art on Horseback," broadcast in the Excursion series, sponsored by the Ford Foundation. And he received word that he would receive an honorary doctorate from his alma mater, Dartmouth (thus making "Dr. Seuss" legitimate).

And, in an article, "Why do Children Bog Down on the First R," in *Life*,[21] John Hersey suggested that someone—perhaps Dr. Seuss—free the nation's children from the oh-so-dreary Dick and Jane readers, which had bored children for years. The idea lay dormant in the back-waters of Dr. Seuss's mind. . . .

But at a party in May of 1954, Helen Geisel was suddenly jolted by pain her feet and ankles. A doctor, Francis M. Smith, offered help, but the Geisels assured him that rest would be all she needed. Two days later, Helen Geisel was checked into the Scripps Metabolic Clinic, as her condition worsened. She had numbness in her arms, hands and face and she could not swallow.[22]

The diagnosis came soon enough: Helen Geisel had Guillian-Barre Syndrome and she was placed in an iron lung. She became unable to speak or sit up without help. She was moved across

San Diego to the San Diego County Hospital, where she was paralyzed from the neck down. She had to have a tracheotomy so she could breathe.

Except for the death of his sister Marnie, Theodor Geisel had always roller-skated through life; he carved out a career with the art that he loved, he lived on a mountain with unlimited physical and equally unlimited professional vistas—tragedy had never really touched him.

Now his wife and helpmate lay near death.

Before the iron lung became available, Guillain-Barre syndrome was fatal; even after iron lungs became available, chances for survival were slight.

Ted Geisel was devastated by the news.

He lived life day by day. He called Dartmouth, saying it would be impossible for him to come to receive his honorary doctorate. And he rigged up a series of mirrors so Helen could see beyond the confines of her iron lung.

He waited.

By the end of June, Helen had rallied. She could again swallow, the paralysis was at least in remission and she improved. She could again attempt speech.

She was moved to the California Rehabilitation Center in Santa Monica for extensive therapy. The Geisel's La Jolla home was, in effect, closed. Theodor Geisel was faced with a multitude of daily tasks Helen had always handled—he really didn't know how to handle a checkbook—or even make coffee. "Helen had always shielded him from the real world," a friend, Elin Vanderlip said.[23]

Slowly, ever so slowly, she learned how to live again.

In August, they received their first copies of *Horton Hears a Who!* and the positive reviews helped buoy their spirits.

Some critics caught Seuss's moral, others didn't.

> The verses are full of the usual lively, informal language and amazing rhymes that have delighted such a

> world-wide audience in the good "doctor's" other books. The story, with its moral, does not match the gayety of some of the older books. But the pictures are as wildly original and funny as ever.
>
> —L. Bechtel, Book Review section
> *The New York Herald Tribune*[24]

> Silly rhymes and limpid pictures, those products of a wonderful imagination, make the story tops in excitement, too.
>
> —*Kirkus*[25]

Jane Cobb, writing in *The New York Times* plaintively says Dr. Seuss is beyond her ability to describe:

> It is probably the most morale tale since the first "Elsie Dinsmore," but since it is written and illustrated by Dr. Seuss it is a lot more fun . . . Children, parents, relatives and friends need not come whimpering to this reviewer to find out what the Whos and their town look like. She knows the limits of her powers of description.[26]

By September, Helen was feeling well enough to move back to their La Jolla home, but she couldn't be left alone. She had a mandatory regimen of exercises to perform every day; she took daily rides on a stationary bicycle, enlivened by her imagination: "I'm en route from Gallup, New Mexico to Shriprock, through the Navajo country, but am running into many detours and sheep . . ."[27]

Brightness returned to both Geisels; for *Colliers* magazine, Ted wrote "A Prayer for a Child" with remarkable simplicity of style:

> From here on earth,
> From my small place

I ask of You
Way out in space:
Please tell all men
In every land
What you and I
Both understand. . . .

Theodor Geisel next turned to the alphabet for *On Beyond Zebra!*, which follows Conrad Cornelius o'Donald o'Dell, who doesn't know that there are letters past Z:

The un-named friend of Conrad Cornelius o'Donald o'Dell (who narrates the book) then invents 20 new letters to follow Z: Yuzz; Wum; Um; Humpf; Fuddle; Glikk; Nuh; Snee; Quan; Thnad; Spazz; Floob; Zatz; Jogg; Flunn; Itch; Yekk; Vroo; Hi! and a final leter which has no name (he asks each reader to name it). Each is shown in fancy calligraphy, with a slightly near-eastern look. The book echoes every child who has ever drawn his or her own alphabet letters on paper (or on the walls at home if mother isn't watching).

Like the stanza about the Ziffs who live on cliffs and the Zuffs who live on bluffs in *Scrambled Eggs Super!*, Dr. Seuss again offers a stanza which is so convoluted that it wraps back upon itself, much like a Mobius strip:

And HUH is the letter I use to spell Nutches
Who live in small caves, known as Nitches, for hutches.
These Nutches have troubles, the biggest of which is
The fact there are many more Nutches than Nitches.
Each Nutch in a Nitch knows that some other Nutch
Would like to move into his Nitch very much.
So each Nutch in a Nitch has to watch that small Nitch
Or Nutches who haven't got Nitches will snitch.[29]

The book ends with Conrad Cornelius o'Donald o'Dell convinced that there is more to the alphabet than A to Z.

He dedicated the book simply: To Helen.

Reviews matched those of other Dr. Seuss books:

> Squirely-que, pluperfect, misty and bewildered pictures accompany each of the new categories.
>
> —Kirkus[30]

> For the fun of it all is in the ridiculous word play, even more inventive this time than in his other recent rhymes. As for the beasts, it is incredible, but he has dreamed up still more, large and small, male and female, each somehow connected with a feeling you yourself wish you could have put into a new word.
>
> —L. B., Book Review section,
> *The New York Herald Tribune*[31]

> Without the Seuss letters there would be no way to spell the names of creatures who look like brooms, or who live in tiny hutches, or who like to sing in grottos. What these creatures look like is indescribable, but they are delightful and it is difficult to imagine how we ever managed without them.
>
> —Jane Cobb, *The New York Times*[32]

A year after the first painful beginning of Helen's Guillain-Barre syndrome, Ted and Helen traveled to Dartmouth College, where, on the thirtieth anniversary of his graduation, he received an honorary doctorate (as did Robert Frost). Geisel was overjoyed to have Helen with him, healthy enough to fly to New Hampshire. The celebration, in May, 1955, was a sweet satisfaction for Geisel, who doubtless remembered the statement he made to his father years earlier, that he was going to Oxford to get a graduate degree. Now he had the degree, honorary though it was. He maintained typical Seussian equilibrium; he was not only Dr. Seuss, he was, as he laughed, "Dr. Dr. Seuss." The gown he wore at the Dartmouth ceremonies he brought with him from the west coast—where he had bought it in a San Diego second-hand store.[33]

Serendipity.

Serendipity drew him then to Boston, where he met William Spaulding, then head of the Education Division of the publishing firm, Houghton Mifflin. Geisel had met Spaulding in Washington during the war; Geisel knew the then-popular book by Rudolf Flesch, *Why Johnny Can't Read*—and he also remembered the article by John Hersey, "Why Do Students Get Bogged Down on First R?" in *Life*, in which Hersey pleaded for better children's books with illustrations by such geniuses as "Tenniel, Howard Pyle, Dr. Seuss, Walt Disney."

Spaulding wanted Geisel to write a book children simply couldn't put down. But Spaulding offered a caveat—he wanted Geisel to use no more than 225 words. Geisel was intrigued with the possibility, but there was a problem. Geisel was bound contractually to Random House. Spaulding would have to somehow work with Bennett Cerf to satisfactorily obtain Dr. Seuss.

Spaulding did so—in a unique way: Spaulding and Bennett Cerf agreed to cut the book fifty-fifty: Houghton Mifflin would publish an educational version of the Dr. Seuss book; Random House would have the "trade rights." In other words, Houghton Mifflin would have the rights to sell the book in schools; Random House would publish the same book and sell it through the "book trade" to bookstores and any other non-educational outlets. It was an ideal method for Spaulding to obtain a Dr. Seuss title; the agreement allowed Bennett Cerf to keep Geisel satisfied and still keep him in the Random House stable.

The book had to wait; Geisel was committed to work on another Random House book: *If I Ran the Circus*.

Patterned after *If I Ran the Zoo*, the book was dedicated:

This Book is for My Dad
Big Ted of Springfield
The Finest Man I'll Ever Know.

It began in typical Seussian fashion, with Morris McGurk dreaming of what a circus he could build behind Sneelock's Store:

Circus lacks something of the pizzazz of *If I Ran the Zoo*, but then again, most sequels rarely match the original. Some critics, who read both books, saw that.

> This Dr. Seuss creation does not start with so bizarre a premise as some of his other extravaganzas. The idea of a small boy dreaming up an ideal circus is not in itself startling. However when the great man gets going, he turns on his own free-wheeling fantasy, which is both peculiar to himself and just plain peculiar. It is also just plain wonderful.
>
> —Jane Cobb, *The New York Times*[35]

> Fantastic animals and people drawn in the familiar Seuss manner—this time in yellow, blues and pinks—with tongue-twisting names and rhymes, make this a book adults and children of all ages will enjoy.
>
> —Norma Rathbun, *The Saturday Review of Literature*[36]

> This is a superb fantasy from that talented purveyor of nonsense in rhyme with excruciatingly funny pictures that will amuse children and anyone else who opens this book.
>
> —San Francisco Chronicle[37]

> A howling Seuss phantasmagoria . . . Four-to-eight-year-old youngsters will agree that "no other circus is half the great circus the Circus McGurkus is."
>
> —K. T. Kinkead, *The New Yorker*[38]

> Small fry may be happy just poring over the pictures, but we suspect that parents will demand that they be permitted to read aloud from Dr. Seuss' delicious verse.
> —M. M. R., *The Chicago Sunday Tribune*[39]

With *If I Ran the Circus* completed, Geisel was able to turn his attention to the challenge of the Spaulding-Cerf, Houghton Mifflin-Random House collaboration, the book that would be better than the best reader any American school child ever saw.

It was nearly an impossible task for Theodor Geisel and nearly an impossible task for Dr. Seuss.

The book took him a full year.

He examined the problem from every angle, gave every word the evil-eye, considered every possible combination of words, pictures, logic, plot. He thought he had a story going with a "Queen Zebra," but discovered neither the words *queen* or *zebra* were in the word list provided.[40] The only job more difficult was, he said, "when I wrote the Baedeker guide Eskimos use when they travel in Siam."[41]

Finally, finally, he saw what he wanted:

> I read (the list) forty times and got more and more discouraged. It was like trying to make strudel without any strudels. I was desperate, so I decided to read it once more. The first two words that rhymed would be the title of my book and I'd go from there. I found "cat" and then I found "hat." That's genius, you see![42]

Five

1956–1960

" . . . easily the best Christmas-cad since Scrooge . . ."

Simply stated, matching *cat* and *hat* revolutionized children's literature.

While he worked and he wrote, he thought and he thought, he began drawing the cat and eventually the cat was born, wearing a red-and-white striped top hat. And it had a red bow tie—note that the tie has three loops, not two. And (perhaps with a bow to Mickey Mouse, at least Mickey in the early cartoons) the cat wore white gloves.

And, as others working with words and pictures can imagine, the cat began to dominate the story. Born in Dr. Seuss's La Jolla dream works, the cat became real—jaunty, perhaps even outrageous. It had a personality and a mind of its own. And it had a smile not unlike the curious smile on the Mona Lisa.

The cat began to carry the story. The narrative began to flow. The story unfolded. It didn't quite have Dr. Seuss's usual galloping anapestic tetrameter, but the rhyme carried the story. And all the words were simple, those in the list Geisel was commanded to use.

Dr. Seuss shows two children, without Mother (or Father), which is an important key to the story. (All we know is that "Mother is out of the house for the day"—no mention of Father.)

And To Think That I Saw It on Mulberry Street and other Dr. Seuss books begin with a daydream: Marco imagines greater and greater sights on Mulberry Street; Gerald McGrew imagines greater and more fantastic animals for his Zooski McGrewski . . . but the Cat in the Hat simply appears. There is no daydream—suddenly he is there.

> And we saw him!
> The Cat in the Hat!
> And he said to us,
> "Why do you sit there like that?"
>
> "I know it is wet
> And the sun is not sunny.
> But we can have
> Lots of good fun that is funny!"[1]

Lots of good fun that is funny clearly means, to the children, the kind of fun without parents that quickly gets out of the child's control. Children, like puppies, can run amok if they are unchecked; lots of good fun that is funny, is clearly fun run amok. And it's the Cat who is the culprit.

In *The Cat in the Hat*, Seuss uses a device as old as storytelling and folklore itself—the trickster figure. The Cat is clearly magical (he appears instantly), as magical as ancient and modern creatures, such as Kokopelli, the trickster figure of the American Indian southwest. The trickster does not think logically; rather it thinks illogically, never planning, using rules all its own, depending on magic to turn events its way. The trickster Cat very much appeals to the sense of rebellion in all children, who secretly wish the world would run their way; who secretly wish they could make the world turn their way by magic.

But the trickster Cat's behavior is counter-balanced by the rigidity of the real world (the world of adults)—the children are constantly worried about what would happen if their mother would return and find the house in such chaos. Indeed, it's every child's nightmare that they will demolish their house only to find Mother at the front door at the worst possible moment.

The Cat in the Hat is one of the greatest topsy turvy trickster stories in all of children's literature (a *bouleversement*, in the French).

The Dr. Seuss illustrations clearly show pandemonium ready to erupt. The children's pet goldfish tries to warn the children and slow down the Cat, but to no avail.

But the Cat begins to juggle a fishbowl (with the goldfish in it) on top of his umbrella, then balances on a ball, with umbrella and goldfish bowl balanced on one gloved hand and a book balanced on the other gloved hand. A teacup teeters precariously on the edge of his top hat. (A reference to the mad tea party in *Alice in Wonderland*, perhaps?)

Then he adds another book balanced on top of the first, a birthday cake hanging at an angle from his top hat, still balanced on one leg on the ball, the other furry foot holding a glass and bottle of milk.

The boy and girl watch the Cat from the very bottom left corner of that page. Children see and read differently, so Dr. Seuss knows to add details, small animals or characters—this time the main characters, the two children—at the far edge of the page. Children's literature critic and authority Karla Kuskin offers an analysis why children see what they see and why their eyes look at books differently:

> The rhythm in a picture book—the way words and pictures move from page to page—is often paced theatrically. In the planning stage a picture book, like film, particularly animated film, is done in storyboard form. The rough illustrations are laid out

> and matched to the appropriate words. These storyboards resemble comic strips, usually minus the word balloons. A baby crawling from frame to frame or a dog playing hide and seek from page to page contribute to the rhythm a picture book needs to keep readers involved and turning the pages. It is also not surprising that such minor characters are also common in animated film and comic strips; they may not say much but they catch young eyes and move things along. The littlest animal tumbling after all the others is almost a Disney trademark. Pogo had a puppy. And Snoopy, who over time made the jump from bit player to the big leagues, has Woodstock, his own silent observer, who in turn has his own groupies, that bunch of birds.[2]

But everything comes falling down with a crash. Everything is a mess and the children know the house shouldn't be like that when Mother returns. The goldfish scolds the Cat for making a huge mess, but the Cat says he knows an even better game. He goes out the door and returns with a big box.

And as the children look on, out popped Thing One and Thing Two, small creatures in red suits with greenish hair. (They have Thing 1 and Thing 2 on their chests and backs.) Sally and the boy narrator don't know what to do upon encountering them, except to fall back on their manners.

The Cat assures the children that the Things are harmless; but they began to fly kites inside the house, knocking down pictures, tables, vases, a chair and ruining their mother's good dress. But the goldfish sees their mother is coming, so the children make desperate efforts to catch the Things with a net. The Cat takes them away in the red box with the hook, but the house is a shambles. Everything is knocked over, wrecked, destroyed.

But the Cat returns with a cleaning vehicle, equipped with arms and hands to pick up and straighten everything.

The Cat in the Hat ends much like *And to Think That I Saw It on Mulberry Street*—do we (children) tell our parents what went on in our world today? Dr. Seuss lets his young readers decide.

Dr. Seuss illustrated the book solely in red and a greenish-bluish color.

The Cat in the Hat proved to be an instant success. It was a success because it was everything a Dick-and-Jane reader shouldn't be: it was written from the child's point of view; it encouraged or espoused random mayhem; parents were not in control; it taught no real moral lesson.

But children could read it by themselves; they could enjoy reading without supervision.

Boxed into the parameters of the word list supplied him, Dr. Seuss created an enduring and engaging character in the Cat in the Hat and created a whole new genre of children's literature. And just as suddenly the Dick and Jane readers were obsolete.

The Cat in the Hat became a publishing phenomenon:

> As soon as the first cartons of *The Cat in the Hat* reached stores, Random House recognized the omens that publishers live for. At Bullock's in Los Angeles, the first 100-copy order disappeared in a day and a hurried call went out for a 250-copy reorder. The Random House trade edition quickly outran Houghton Mifflin's school edition, averaging sales at the start of about twelve thousand copies a month and rising rapidly. The book escalated into a sensation: spurred by playground word-of-mouth, children nagged their parents to buy it. "Parents," Ted said, "understand better than school people the necessity for this kind of reader." Within three years *Cat* sold nearly a million copies at $1.95 each, with editions in French, Chinese, Swedish and Braille,

Geisel's biographers Judith and Neil Morgan said. (The copy I have indicates the 99th reprinting . . . [3])

Critics fell in love with the book and the mischievous cat as quickly as children did:

> It's fine, furious slapstick, told in rolling rhythms and lots of conversation. Dr. Seuss has used only 223 different words, according to the publisher, and according to my count, less than a dozen of these are two-syllable, all chosen for an eye to the knowledge and ability of the first and second grade reader. And there are Dr. Seuss' own illustrations to help make this one of the most original and funniest of books for early readers.
>
> —E. L. Buell, *The New York Times*[4]

> "The Cat in the Hat" is elegant nonsense. We were afraid that the limitations Dr. Seuss put upon himself might have shackled his marvelous inventiveness. Quite the contrary.
>
> —M. S. Libby, Book Review section, *The New York Herald Tribune*[5]

> All the old delightful rimes and rhythms, the zany illustrations are here. Together they make a book to rejoice 7 and 8 year olds and make them look with distinct disfavor on the drab adventures of standard primer characters.
>
> —P.G., *The Chicago Sunday Tribune*[6]

> Here is the same delicious nonsense, hilarious fun, cumulative build-up, and surprise ending that distinguish one of America's most original picture books, "And To Think That I Saw It on Mulberry Street."
>
> —H. A. M., *The Saturday Review of Literature*[7]

> Recommended enthusiastically as a picture book as well as a reader. Complete departure from the usual dull and unimaginative books of this type.
>
> —*Bookmark*[8]

And then, the Cat established a publishing house. Alone it would have been substantial; inside Random House, it fortified Random's reputation as one of the premiere publishing houses for children's books.

Phyllis Cerf, Bennett Cerf's wife, took Geisel to lunch the next time he visited New York and the Random House headquarters. She reminded him that years previously, when he was working on the Flit campaigns, they worked together. She had worked at the McCann-Eriksson advertising agency and although Geisel produced all his Flit illustrations at home, when he wanted space at the agency, the space provided was her desk.

She suggested that, as big as the success of *The Cat in the Hat* was, it could be ever bigger. She proposed that Dr. Seuss begin a series of similar books. He could produce Dr. Seuss books in a bigger format, using a more complex vocabulary; books such as *The Cat in the Hat* could and should be completed using much the same basic vocabulary which Geisel/Dr. Seuss wrestled with before discovering *cat* and *hat.*

Thus was born Beginner books, a publishing house inside a publishing house (a room within the Random House house, if you will). Geisel and Phyllis—and Helen—would hold portions of the stock (later smaller portions were given to Bennett Cerf and even later, smaller shares in the firm were given to others at Random House).

Ensconced in his La Jolla Tower, Geisel put aside the idea of the new series to work on another Dr. Seuss book he had promised Random House.

And as big as *The Cat in the Hat* had become, this would become even bigger. (*. . . And so forth and upward and onward, gee whiz!*)

For the first time, the focus in a Dr. Seuss book would be, not a boy, but an adult; and the focus was on not on good but a villain. As many children might say, "a bad guy."

The Grinch.

Dr. Seuss was not averse to borrowing characters from one book to use again in another. That only meant that his young readers were familiar with the character and would more easily accept a new book. So he had Marco from *And to Think That I Saw It on Mulberry Street* reappear in *McElligot's Pool* ; and he had Bartholomew from *The 500 Hats of Bartholomew Cubbins* reappear in *Bartholomew and the Oobleck.*

So he let the Whos from Whoville reappear in this book. And he pictured the Grinch's personality with a remarkably apt description (which even children—maybe especially children—could understand):

> The Grinch *hated* Christmas! The whole Christmas season
> Now, please don't ask why. No one quite knows the reason.
> It *could* be his head wasn't screwed on just right.
> It *could* be, perhaps, that his shoes were too tight.
> But I think that the most likely reason of all
> May have been that his heart was two sizes too small.[9]

And with that beginning, Dr. Seuss created a fable just as charming as *'Twas the Night Before Christmas* and just as enduring as *A Christmas Carol*. The library service *Kirkus* called the Grinch "easily the best Christmas-cad since Scrooge."

The Grinch hated the Whos's presents and toys, feasting, and joy and singing and NOISE! He says he has tolerated Christmas for 53 years.

(Theodor Geisel was 53 years old when he wrote, and Random House published, *How The Grinch Stole Christmas!)*

The Grinch tied antlers to his dog Max, harnessed him to a sleigh, donned a Santa suit and, on Christmas Eve, like a perverse, reverse Santa Clause, went down a *Who* chimney and took all the presents, all the meats, all the treats, all the feasts. And even their Christmas tree. He was caught, by little Cindy-Lou *Who*, "who was no more than two." She asked "Santy Claus, why, *WHY* are you taking our Christmas tree? WHY?"

The Grinch lied: "a bulb is out—I am taking it to my workshop and I'll bring it right back here."

He returned to the top of Mount Crumpet; with his sledload to dump it, expecting to hear the sobs and the cries of the Who children.

But everyone had a joyous Christmas anyway.

It was, perhaps the easiest Dr. Seuss book to write, except for the conclusion. Geisel didn't have a conclusion for the longest time. He explained to Judith and Neil Morgan how the conclusion came to be:

> I got hung up getting the Grinch out of the mess. I got into a situation where I sounded like a second-rate preacher or some biblical truism. . . . Finally in desperation . . . without making any statement whatever, I showed the Grinch and the Whos together at the table, and making a pun of the Grinch carving "the roast beast" . . . I had gone through thousands of religious choices, and then after three months it came out like that.[10]

Dr. Seuss added a name and virtually a dictionary definition to our culture:

> Grinch: any sour, pessimistic person who dismisses love and attempts to deprive others of happiness..

And the hard GR sound of Grinch is just perfect.

(Some newspaper headline writers and critics of Speaker of the House Newt Gingrich have linked his name, and perceived negative House of Representatives acts, to the Grinch: "The Gingrich Who. . . .")

Dr. Seuss made a strong moral in Bartholomew and the Oobleck:

> Sometimes you have to say *I'm Sorry,*
> Sometimes you have to say *It's my fault,*
> Even if you're a king.

And he made a strong moral point in *Horton Hears a Who:*

> A person's a person, no matter how small.

And he taught an even bigger lesson, about the nation's biggest celebration, in *How the Grinch Stole Christmas!*:

> Maybe Christmas doesn't come from a store.
> Maybe Christmas . . . means a little bit more!

It was a Dr. Seuss lesson not lost on children and certainly not lost on their parents.

While *The Cat in the Hat* was still setting sales records, the first printing the *Grinch* was 50,000 copies.[11]

And the critics raved:

> The inimitable Dr. Seuss has brought off a fresh triumph in his new picture book . . . The verse is as lively and the pages are as bright and colorful as anyone could wish. Reading the book aloud will be a fascinating exercise for parents or for older brothers and sisters, who will pretend they are entertaining the children while secretly enjoying the humor and the moral for themselves.
>
> —A. O'B. M. *The Saturday Review of Literature*[12]

> Wonderful fantasy, in the true Dr. Seuss manner, with pictures in the Christmas colors.
>
> —Charlotte Jackson, *The San Francisco Chronicle*[13]

> Even if you prefer Dr. Seuss in a purely antic mood, you must admit that if there's a moral to be pointed out, no one can do it more gaily. The reader is swept along by the ebullient rhymes and the weirdly zany pictures until he is limp with relief when the Grinch reforms and, like the latter, mellow with good feeling.
>
> —E. L. B., *The New York Times*[14]

> His peculiar and original genius in line and word is always the same, yet, so rich are the variations he plays on his themes, always fresh and amusing.
>
> —M.S. Libby, Book Review section,
> *The New York Herald Tribune*[15]

And the *Kirkus* service, which recognized the Grinch as a modern-day Scrooge:

> Youngsters will be in transports over the goofy gaiety of Dr. Seuss's first book about a villain—easily the best Christmas-cad since Scrooge. Inimitable Seuss illustrations of the Grinch's dog Max disguised as a reindeer are in black and white with touches of red. Irrepressible and irresistible.
>
> —*Kirkus*[16]

In New York, Phyllis Cerf compiled a list of 379 words, from which a Beginner Books author could choose 200, plus 20 "emergency" words for each book project.[17]

In California, Beginner Books was housed in Helen's office, formerly a garage at the Geisel's La Jolla aerie. Above her desk was a gift from Phyllis Cerf: a needlepoint portrait of The Cat in the Hat, inscribed:

THIS CAT STARTED A PUBLISHING HOUSE. NO OTHER CAT CAN MAKE THIS CLAIM.[18]

Beginner Books borrowed money from Random House to finance the start-up; the new company may have started well, for a while, but Phyllis Cerf and Ted Geisel soon clashed on the projects the firm would publish; she was a fighter, he wasn't; he demanded (politely) rules for the books which Dr. Seuss had learned the hard, *very* hard way over the years and through the past books. All his rules made perfect sense, in terms of children's books, especially preschool books:

* Only one picture per page;

* The text should never mention anything that wasn't illustrated;

* Pages which faced each other should be inter-locked, so the two pages form one unit, i.e., if page one is the first right-hand page, then pages 2 and 3 are facing pages and the pictures and text for those pages should be a single unit.[19]

As mild-mannered as Ted Geisel was, few other authors could meet his style demands. And thus Beginner Books was often in a collective quandary and without suitable book projects to put into production. Book projects by Truman Capote and Nathaniel Benchley were both rejected by the Beginner Books triumverate.[20]

Robert Bernstein was hired by Random House from Simon & Schuster to help satisfy the public demand for Dr. Seuss; Ted Geisel's plaintive question of only several years earlier, "Can I make five thousand dollars a year on my work" was beginning to be answered, YES, YES, YES because of the post-war baby boom. No one could have anticipated the baby boom and the thousands of children who would "grow into" Dr. Seuss books each year. Not to mention Dr. Seuss books which were bought, colored in with crayons, bought by schools and community libraries and lost by small tykes and then replaced by other copies. Bernstein fueled the Dr. Seuss boom by making sure there were a few, but only a few Dr. Seuss toys, just as Disney had learned to do with Mickey Mouse lunchpails, Mickey Mouse watches (which appreciated hugely in value over the years) Disney "snowdomes" and a vast, never-ending cornucopia of Mickey Mouse-Donald Duck, Disneyiana.

As reluctant as he was to travel, Geisel appeared on behalf of his books during a ten-day marketing blitz during the 1958 holiday season included Boston, Rochester, Washington, D.C.; Chicago; Madison, Wisconsin and Cleveland. Dr. Seuss was mobbed at each stop.

Dr. Seuss returned to his La Jolla desk and completed *The Cat in the Hat Comes Back* and, like *If I Ran the Circus*, it was good Dr. Seuss, which meant that it was light years better than anything everybody else was publishing, but it wasn't *inspired* Dr. Seuss. But critics still appreciated it, nearly almost as much as the original *(98 and 3/4th percent guaranteed. . . .)*

> While not as rib-tickling as the first story, this one is still well above the average book for beginning readers both in imaginativeness and humor and in narrative and pictorial interest. First graders should be able to read it by themselves.
>
> —*Booklist*[21]

> Using only 252 different words, culled from a beginning reader's list, (Dr. Seuss) tells in hilarious verse and outrageously funny pictures the further adventures of a couple of youngsters and a naughty cat.
>
> —E.C. Mann, *The Chicago Sunday Tribune*[22]

> A top-notch sequel to "The Cat in the Hat," providing delightful fare for beginning readers. . . .
>
> —B. M. Doh, *Library Journal*[23]

> It may be awkwardly rhymed in spots and limited by only 252 different words, but the nonsense and

> spontaneous fun of Dr. Seuss is here for the first and second graders to read.
>
> —*Wisconsin Library Bulletin*[24]

> The chief difficulty with the new series of "Beginner Books". . . . (is) the problem of keeping misguided parents, teachers and older children (who enjoy them immensely) from reading them aloud to children who have not yet begun to read and so spoiling all the fun and profit for them.
>
> —M. S. Libby, Book Review section,
> *The New York Herald Tribune*[25]

And to Ted Geisel's pleasure, we can be sure, Beginner Books published *A Fly Went By*, by Marshall "Mike" McClintock, his Dartmouth friend who met him on a Manhattan Street all those years ago, took him into the offices of The Vanguard Press and agreed to publish *And To Think That I Saw It on Mulberry Street.* ("*. . . an elephant's faithful, one hundred percent . . .*")

As of late summer, 1997, *A Fly Went By* is still in print with Beginner Books, now in its 55th reprinting.

In 1957, Helen Geisel suffered dizziness and confusion and was taken to the Scripps Clinic; she was diagnosed as having suffered a small stroke. She was back at home several days later, with slight problems in her right hand and right side and lacking her usual self.

While Random House was putting *The Cat in the Hat* and *The Cat in the Hat Comes Back* into production, Theodor Geisel began working on another Dr. Seuss project. It was the first time he would combine three shorter stories into one book: *Yertle the Turtle and Other Stories*. The other stories were "Gertrude McFuzz" and "The Big Brag."

With the story "Yertle the Turtle" Dr. Seuss posed another major moral; children understood the story, but many children (*and* adults) missed the moral:

> They *were* . . . until Yertle, the king of them all,
> decided the kingdom he ruled was too small.
> "I'm ruler," said Yertle, "of all I can see.
> "But I can't see *enough*. That's the trouble with me
> With this stone for a throne, I look down on my pond
> But I can not look down on the places beyond.
> This throne that I sit on is too, too low down.
> It ought to be *higher*!" he said with a frown.
> "If I could sit high, how much greater I'd be!
> What a king! I'd be ruler of all I could see!"

So turtles and more turtles and more turtles came and they all climbed on the back of a turtle named Mack, until the pile of turtles grew higher and higher. And Yertle, the King Turtle, could see longer and farther and he was King of all he could see.

And Yertle the King Turtle ordered even more turtles to climb onto the stack, to heighten the stack even more on Mack's back. (Yet he was offended that the moon was higher than he.)

But Mack got tired of being on the bottom and he protested with a "burp!" and the stack came tumbling down.

And what was the moral? That all turtles and all creatures should be free. And on what was it based? Ted Geisel explained the story to Cynthia Gorney, of *The Washington Post*, in May, 1979:

> La Jolla, Calif.—One afternoon in 1957, as he bent over the big drawing board in his California studio, Theodor Seuss Geisel found himself drawing a turtle.
>
> He was not sure why.
>
> He drew another turtle and saw that it was underneath the first turtle, holding him up.
>
> He drew another, and another, until he had an enormous pileup of turtles, each standing on the back of the turtle below it and hanging its turtle head, looking pained.

> Geisel looked at this turtle pile. He asked himself, not unreasonably, What does this mean? Who is the turtle on top?
>
> Then he understood that the turtle on top was Adolf Hitler.
>
> "I couldn't draw Hitler as a turtle," Geisel says, now hunched over the same drawing board, making pencil scribbles of the original yertle the Turtle drawings as he remembers them. "So, I drew him as King What-ever-his-name-was, King" (Scribble) "of the Pond." (Scribble.) "He wanted to be King as far as he could see. So kept piling them up. He conquered Central Europe and France, and there it was."
>
> (Scribble.)
>
> "Then I had this great pileup, and I said, 'How do you get rid of this impostor?'
>
> "Believe it or not," I said, 'The voice of the people.' I said, 'Well, I'll just simply have the guy on the bottom burp.'"[26]

Yertle the Turtle was Dr. Seuss's answer to depotism: Fascism and Nazism.

It was as important a moral as *a person's a person, no matter how small,* in *Horton Hears a Who!*

And Theodor Geisel had to fight long and hard to get that single *burp!* into a Random House book.

> A must for both remedial reading and reading aloud. The sweeping illustrations and the spontaneous verse of these three stories make them a welcome addition to that nonsensical, but wise, world of the always popular Dr. Seuss.
>
> —*Kirkus*[27]

> Dr. Seuss' talent in using ordinary, simple words with vividness, humor and unflagging rhythm, coupled

with his ability to draw eloquently funny illustrations, make his stories easily readable for young children and equally enjoyable for many a well-read adult.

—E. D., *The Horn Book Magazine*[28]

Hurray! Three shining examples of Dr. Seuss' unique art, first published in a magazine, are now out in a book, pointing little morals for our delight and profit. . . . A hilarious addition to the Dr. Seuss shelf.

—P. G., *The Chicago Sunday Tribune*[29]

This three-in-one chuckle bargain in hard covers is sure to delight Dr. Seuss fans, even though they will not regard it as the super-colossal accomplishment characteristic of many of Seuss's more recent extravaganzas.

—Della McGregor, *The Saturday Review of Literature*[30]

As much as Dr. Seuss books were bought by libraries for year upon year of children growing into the reading level of the books, Geisel so far had missed an obvious target: even as *a person's a person, not matter how small*, his next book captured a guaranteed market: *everyone has a birthday, no matter how old.*

So he completed *Happy Birthday to You!* with most of the inside right front cover blank so parents can sign, date and give the book to the birthday boy or birthday girl.

Critics of all ages loved it:

Any child lucky enough to be flown to Katroo on Smorgasbord's back will be reduced to a happy state of hypnosis by the skillful rhymes and Seussian pictures.

—Charlotte Jackson, *The Atlantic Monthly*[32]

The better a child's book is, the more completely it must turn topsy turvy all the characteristic style and attitudes of the school reader—the stammering prose,

> the didactic realism of the illustrations, the family relationships, the role of the animal, the unquestioning adjustment to petty bourgeois morals and manners.
>
> —Elizabeth Kilbourn, *The Canadian Forum*[33]

> This multicolored excursion is a gay and festive one, though perhaps a little too long and involved. The rhyming text and imaginative illustrations, however, will delight not only Dr. Seuss fans, but birthday boys and girls as well.
>
> —N. B. Childs, *Library Journal*[34]

While he, Helen and Phyllis Cerf squabbled over possibilities for the Beginner Books list, and before *Happy Birthday to You!* was published, Ted and Helen took a quick vacation and returned to his studio to begin yet another Beginner Book, *One Fish Two Fish Red Fish Blue Fish.*

It was smaller in volume, like *The Cat in the Hat* and used the restricted word list, which Dr. Seuss mastered in *The Cat in the Hat.*

One Fish Two Fish Red Fish Blue Fish begins with fish, then continues with Seussian animals of every size, shape and variety. Some have their names on their chests (Mike, Clark); others only identified by Seussian species: a Wump; a Nook; a Zans; a Ying; a Yop; small yellow fellows called the Zeds; an Ish; a Gak, a Zeep.

The most famous creature in *Red Fish Blue Fish . . .* may be the bear-like Gox, shown wearing yellow boxing gloves, boxing with the narrator, a small boy:

> I like to box
> How I like to box!
> so, every day,
> I box a Gox.

In yellow socks
I box my Gox
I box in yellow
Gox box socks.[35]

Most critics read *One Fish Two Fish . . .* as simply on a par with other Seuss books:

> The new Dr. Seuss is fun, just plain fun. Not perhaps such a verbal tour de force as "The Cat in the Hat," it is useful for beginning readers. The text, as always with Dr. Seuss, shows more subtlety and variety than his pictures.
>
> —M. S. Libby, Book Review section, *The New York Herald Tribune*[36]

> Easy-to-read but hard-to-fathom pastiche. Seven- and eight-year-olds may be pleased with the frantic humor of this book.
>
> —*The Saturday Review of Literature*[38]

and:

> However much adults may yawn over Dr. Seuss, and sigh over their children's delight, he does seem to know exactly what children just beginning to read find unbearably funny.
>
> —*The Christian Science Monitor*[38]

E. L. Buell, writing in *The New York Times Book Review*, clearly and completely understood what Seuss was doing in *One Fish Two Fish Red Fish Blue Fish. . . .*

> This is not a story but a collection of daffy verses about the daffiest of subjects and situations, done in the

> inimitable Seuss manner, complete with hypnotic rhymes, jokes, a picture-menagerie of Seuss-type animals that never were on land or sea. . . . (This) is designed to ease the reader into an inkling of how phonics work, and in most cases the name is lettered on some prominent part of the animal's anatomy, for quick recognition and word association. Also slipped in are some exercises in counting and recognition of shapes and colors. Of course the great thing about the Seuss books is that they never seem educational, just high-voltage fun to read, to look at and to listen to.[39]

Just as he had done earlier with Smith and Haas, and The Vanguard Press, Bennett Cerf quickly found Beginner Books too valuable to ignore; by April, 1960, it had set exceeded a million dollars in sales.[40] He proposed that Random House simply buy the firm.

The Geisels wasn't terribly interested in that idea; Ted knew that huge profits from the sale would be taxable and thus largely lost. But Cerf suggested a deferred sales plan that would avoid huge taxes; Ted and Helen would continue to run the company. Geisel was an innocent in the world of business, so he acquested to the plan, and invested wisely.

In the process of negotiating about Beginner Books, Cerf offered Geisel a challenge: now that Dr. Seuss could successfully publish a book with about 250 words—could Dr. Seuss write a book with only 50 words?

The bet was $50.

The book was *Green Eggs and Ham*:

> That Sam-I-am!
> That Sam-I-am!
> I do not like
> That Sam-I-am!

Do you like
green eggs and ham?

I do not like them,
Sam-I-am.[41]

Geisel had worked furiously with charts, checklists, notations; his imagination was aided and abetted by pure, unadulterated hard work.

Chuck Jones, creator of Bugs Bunny, clearly saw how Geisel succeeded with *Green Eggs and Ham*: he took the common phrase, *ham and eggs*, and commanded attention by reversing it. Jones compared Geisel's phrasing to that of the Pennsylvania Dutch (who are not Dutch at all, but of German heritage, Dutch being a variation of *Deutsch*, German for *German*), or Yiddish, which used phrases like "He doesn't like opera, my Father" or "throw Mother from the train, a kiss."

Geisel's best, such as *Green Eggs and Ham*, Jones said, "has that quality of puzzlement. He uses Sam-I-am, not just Sam, and Sam-I-am not only rhymes with green-eggs and ham, but has the same metric emphasis."[42]

> Sam-I-am drives his victim crazy, pursuing him everywhere while he urges him to eat something disgusting. Literature has seldom afforded children an opportunity to ally themselves with such open antagonism, Ted was building on the breakthrough of *The Cat in the Hat*, whose boisterous rampage in the absence of adults went unpunished, alarming some of the school establishment who felt safer with Dick and Jane and considered the Cat "a trickster hero."

Judith and Neil Morgan wrote.[43]

Geisel later said it was "the only book I ever wrote that still makes me laugh."[44]

Mary Malone, in the *Library Journal*, wrote:

> Another beginning reader with Dr. Seuss' usual ingenuity in rhyme, telling in a limited vocabulary but unlimited exuberance of illustration, of Sam-I-am who wins a determined campaign to make another Seuss character eat a plate of green eggs and ham.[45]

M.S. Libby, in *The New York Herald Tribune* hit the book dead-on:

> He limits himself to monosyllables, but his pictures and the wonderful dead-pan humor are superb.[46]

Emily Maxwell, in *The New Yorker* wrote:

> Dr. S. can play so many tunes on his simplified keyboard that, reading him, one is hardly aware that there *are* more than fifty words . . . [47]

And *The Saturday Review of Literature* said:

> The happy theme of refusal-to-eat changing to relish will be doubly enjoyable to the child who finds many common edibles as nauseating as the title repast. The pacing throughout is magnificent and the opening five pages, on which the focal character introduces himself with a placard: "I am Sam," are unsurpassed. . . . [48]

And books like *Green Eggs and Ham, Mr. Brown Can Moo! Can You?* and *Marvin K. Mooney, Will You Please Go Now!* remind us that Dr. Seuss is one of the great creators of nonsense verse in the English language—verse in which you can almost hear an unmistakable musical accompaniment, children's literature authority Jonathan Cott wrote, in *Pipers at the Gates of Dawn: The Wisdom of Children's Literature*.[49]

Now in its 99th reprinting, *Green Eggs and Ham* has been presented as a rap song (by the Canadian band Moxy Früvous), and in a memorable occasion, was recited by the Rev. Jesse Jackson, on "Saturday Night Live," as a black minister would intone it during a southern Sunday sermon.

After publication, Theodor Geisel was occasionally presented with plates of green eggs and ham. "Vile stuff," he said.

Six

1960–1971

"And I learned there are troubles of more than one kind. *Some come from ahead and some come from behind.*"

"I'm subversive as hell," Theodor Geisel said and he meant it. Not quite subversive in a totally political sense, but a political sense mixed with literature.

> I've always had a mistrust of adults. And one reason I dropped out of Oxford and the Sorbonne was that I thought they were taking life too damn seriously, concentrating too much on nonessentials. Hilaire Belloc, whose writing I liked a lot, was a radical. *Gulliver's Travels* was subversive and both Swift and Voltaire influenced me. *The Cat in the Hat* is a revolt against authority, but it's ameliorated by the fact that the Cat cleans up everything in the end. It's revolutionary in that it goes as far as Kerensky and then stops. It doesn't go quite as far as Lenin.

* * *

> Children's literature as I write it and as I see it is satire to a great extent—satirizing the mores and the habits of the world. There's *Yertle the Turtle* (about the turtle dictator who becomes "the ruler of all I can see" by sitting on the backs of hundreds of subject turtles, his throne brought down by the simple burp of the lowliest and lowest turtle), which was modeled on the rise of Hitler. . . .[1]

And then he wrote "The Sneetches," which appeared in *The Sneetches and Other Stories*:

> Now, the Star-Belly Sneetches
> Had bellies with stars.
> The Plain Belly Sneetches
> Had none upon thars.
>
> Those stars weren't so big. They were really so small
> You might think such a thing wouldn't matter at all.
>
> But, because they had stars, all the Star-Belly Sneetches
> Would brag, "We're the best kind of Sneetches on the beaches."[2]

Then Sylvester McMonkey McBean, the Fix-it-Up Chappie, arrived with a curious machine: for three dollars each, every Plain Belly Sneetch could enter the machine and come out with a star:

Then McBean said, to the Sneetches with stars, for *ten* dollars, you can enter my machine, which will take off your stars.

And even Theodor Geisel learned a lesson from *The Sneetches and Other Stories*. The last story in the book is "The Empty Pants," in which the narrator, a small child, is scared of an empty pair of pants in the dark:

And then they moved! Those empty pants!
They kind of started jumping.
And then my heart, I must admit,
It kind of started thumping.

So I got out. I got out fast
As fast as I could go, sir.
I wasn't scared. But pants like that
I do not care for. No, sir.[3]

(The empty pants clearly represented an authority figure which didn't have to be feared. . . .)

When Robert Bernstein, publisher at Random House, visited in La Jolla, Ted Geisel has the storyboards for the book on the walls. "I'd decided to abandon the book," he told an astonished Bernstein, "Someone I respect told me it was anti-Semitic."

"The Sneetches" was Geisel's strong statement: he was *against* anti-semitism. Against prejudice. Against bigotry. Against peoples vs. peoples.

During the Holocaust, Jews were forced to wear stars. Dr. Seuss turned that around, and into, the Plain-Belly Sneetches and the Star-Belly Sneetches.

It was as strong a moral as he had in *Yertle the Turtle*, where he avoided drawing Hitler as Yertle the Turtle King, but made the same point about Nazism.

Robert Bernstein talked him out of abandoning *The Sneetches and Other Stories*. And Geisel, himself, discovered that the person—"someone I respect"—who thought the book was anti-semitic was . . . was . . . well, an empty pair of pants in the dark. That Geisel didn't have to be scared of.

"Those spooky pants and I came face to face," he told Bernstein.[4]

One (story) is a hilarious vignette about a mother who named all of her 23 sons Dave. The other three are parables on prejudice, stubbornness, and fear of the

> unknown, thumpingly told in the famous Dr. Seuss style that starts with the absurd and the preposterous and goes on from there.
>
> —Joan Beck, *The Chicago Sunday Tribune*[5]

> The best, "What Was I Scared of" makes an excellent creepy story for Halloween. . . . The title story, while amusing, is rather too obvious in its moral.
>
> —Alice Daigliesh, *The Saturday Review of Literature*[6]

Ted and Helen Geisel began to regret the work load they had to put into Beginner Books. In late 1961, they received a call from Donald Klopfer, at Random House, telling them that he had sold direct mail rights to Grolier, which was beginning a direct mail children's book club. Helen Geisel asked if there were any other books sold to Grolier in addition to Beginner Books. Klopfer said that Harpers had also sold their children's book line to Grolier, for the new book club.

Helen—and Ted—refused. Helen refused first. Grolier would sell Beginner Books solely, or not at all. It was Klopfer's turn to be astonished. Then even more astonished when Grolier accepted the Geisel's polite demand. Forty years later, Grolier had paid more than forty million dollars to Beginner Books, a very, very substantial portion of those royalties were for Dr. Seuss books. And, in the bargain, Grolier has become the biggest and most successful children's book club in the country.[7]

Ted Geisel then resurrected the pseudonym Theo. LeSieg, for some books, in which he would write the text, but others would do the illustrations. *Ten Apples Up on Top*, was the first, in 1961; *I Wish I Had Duck Feet* was published in 1965 and *Come on Over to My House*, in 1966. Others were released after that. They were not quite top-drawer Seuss but they did fit in the Beginner Book series.

The next Dr. Seuss was not a collection of stories, but a book based on every parent's-every evening predicament: how to get the baby or toddler off to sleep.

Dr. Seuss's Sleep Book was published in 1962 and was in the form of a report, who's asleep where. . . .

Ted Geisel works his way into the wonderful convoluted nonsense that matches the very best of the previous Dr. Seuss books:

> But it isn't too good when a moose and a goose
> Start dreaming they're drinking the other one's juice.
> Moose juice, not goose juice, is juice for a moose
> And goose juice, not moose juice, is juice for a goose.
> So, when goose gets a mouthful of juices of moose's
> And moose gets a mouthful of juices of goose's,
> They always fall out of their beds screaming screams.
> SO. . . .[8]

E. L. Buell, writing in *The New York Times Book Review* caught the book perfectly in his first sentence:

> A rarity among books—one deliberately calculated to make its readers yawn. And anyone who has followed Dr. Seuss's twenty-five years career as author-artist knows how persuasive he is. No one could resist those zillions of astonishing sleepyheads . . . which only he could have invented, pictured and described in hypnotic rhythms which bring yawns right on top of the chuckles.[9]

The Christian Science Monitor offered:

> This new Dr. Seuss, hardly a classic, at least has the considerable virtue of being continually silly and unflaggingly inventive . . . Whether the thought of Biffer-Baum Birds and Collapsible Frinks nestling down will promote drowsiness in young humans I do not know. In a test on one seven-year-old, the result was giggling. The drawings are, if anything, more frazzled, more rubbery than ever.
>
> —E. W. Foell[10]

With Beginner Books, Dr. Seuss continued to be "subversive as hell"; his books taught children numbers, phonics, words, relationships. And they were taught so easily, in the form of Dr. Seuss stories and Dr. Seuss creatures, that children didn't know they were learning.

And for the next few years, after *Dr. Seuss's Sleep Book*, Geisel concentrated on Beginner Books, which were promoted with the line on the covers, "The SIMPLEST SEUSS for YOUNGEST USE." But they were no less difficult to write: in fact, the shorter the book, the more difficult and the fewest words available to for Geisel to use, the harder to make a plot line.

For *Hop on Pop*, released in spring, 1963, the good doctor matches simple words and their usage:

> NO
> PAT
> NO
> Don't sit on that.[11]

(Pat, a yellow bear, or yellow Seuss bear-like creature, stands perplexed beside a cactus.)

Dr. Seuss's ABC, released the fall of the same year, uses these forms:

> BIG A
> little a
> What begins with A?
> Aunt Annie's alligator. . . . A . . a . . A.

Critics continued to rave about Beginner Books and *Hop on Pop*:

> As for Dr. Seuss, that wizard is bent on removing reading frustrations before they start and he deserves a

special fanfare for Hop on Pop. . . . The illustrations are as funny as ever; they also provide clues for figuring out the meanings of words. Dr. Seuss thinks of everything.

—E. L. Buell, *The New York Times Book Review*[13]

A hilarious first reader . . . which will captivate even the average six-year-old.

—*Christian Century*[14]

Superb, simple Seuss. Funny, phonetic, fantastic. It groups one syllable rhythmic and rhyming words together, uses them in brief sentences and illustrates the idea hilariously with the Doctor's ever fresh and amusing oddities . . . Try it on your 4-year-old now that it's pedagogically respectable to allows that age to attempt to read! Or forget about teaching them anything and have fun.

—M. S. Libby, Books section,
The New York Herald Tribune[15]

And *Dr. Seuss's ABC* . . .

Dr. Seuss's ABC will be the special joy of all the siblings whose older brethren chuckle happily over the good Doctor's zany creations. Everyone else will benefit from it, too, because it stresses not only the letter, but the sound it makes as it grows into a word.

—Alberta Eiseman, *The New York Times Book Review*[16]

The zany Dr. Seuss may be the despair of many educators ever since his "Cat in the Hat". . . . Whether Dr. Seuss has any purpose or not, or whether a child will learn ABC's by mouthing phrases like "googoo goggles, quacking quacker-oo and Fiffer-feffer-feff" is perhaps beside the point. Children seem to enjoy Seussy sauciness

> and although his googoo goggles gobbledygook may not fulfill all the needs of education it certainly put any fear of letters completely at the mercy of a chubby Zizzer-zazzer-zuzz.
>
> —Guernsey La Pelley
> *The Christian Science Monitor*[17]

Bennett Cerf and all his colleagues at Random House came to expect a Seuss title annually, automatically. Lulled into a half-false sense of security about the good doctor laboring away in his tower in La Jolla, Seuss jolted them by adding clearly non-Seussian rhymes, which had to be edited out. *Hop on Pop* went to New York with these lines:

> When I read I am smart
> I always cut whole words apart.
> Con Stan Tin O Ple, Tim Buk Too
> Con Tra Cep Tive, Kan Ga Roo.[18]

The final book read:

> My father
> can read
> big words, too.
> Like . . .
>
> Constantinpole
> and
> Timbuktu[19]

Later, in *Fox in Sox*, Geisel tried using:

> Moe blows Joe's nose
> Joe blows Moe's nose.

And Bennett Cerf and Random House wouldn't go for *that*, either.[20]

The front cover of the next Dr. Seuss book, *Fox in Sox*, carries this admonition:

> This is a book you READ ALOUD to find out just how smart your tongue is. The first time you read it, don't go fast! This Fox is a tricky fox. He'll try to get your tongue in trouble.

Indeed.

The book is a dialogue between Fox, who is a red fox, and Knox, who is a yellow bear-like creature.

Try these Seussian lines from *Fox in Sox:*

> Through three cheese trees
> three free fleas flew.
> While these fleas flew,
> freezy breeze blew.[21]

Couldn't say it, could you? Neither can I.

The New York Times reviewers were always on Seuss's side; as was *The Christian Science Monitor:*

> Tongue trippers . . . from the facile mind and humorous pen of Dr. Seuss . . . Let the beginners read and recite with sly Fox (in sox) the simple words which always accumulate into audible pandemonium. It will be a rigorous and riotous trip.
>
> —G. A. Woods, *The New York Times Book Review*[22]

> (A second-grader) wrote: "I like the pictures. I think sometimes you get mixed up. I think it is funny. I like the words and rhymes and words that sound alike." This confirmed a parental impression that a

> young reader will persist in something new and different—even tongue-twisters like these—if there are pleasures to pull him along. Dr. Seuss, involved here with tweetle beetles in a puddle paddle battle, continues to supply such pleasures.
>
> —Roderick Nordell, *The Christian Science Monitor*[25]

His next book, a larger Dr. Seuss book, rather than a smaller Beginner Book, also spoke with a loud voice with a clear moral.

I Had Trouble In Getting to Solla Sollew is Dr. Seuss's most pessimistic book. (It may have been Dr. Seuss somehow speaking to Theodor Geisel.)

> I was real happy and carefree and young
> and I lived in a place called the Valley of Vung
> And nothing, not anything ever went wrong
> Until . . . well, one day I got walking along. . . .

He meets trouble after trouble on the way . . .

He continues through a storm, a flood, and encounters the army of . . . General Genghis Kahn Schmitz, who is forced to retreat facing the ominous Army of the Perilous Poozer of Pompelmoose Pass.[24]

Finally, the narrator gets to Solla Sollew, but the doorkeeper admitted one small trouble: the door is locked and a Key-Slapping Slippard always knocks the key out of the door. And they can't get into Solla Sollew.

The key to the book was:

> And I learned there are troubles
> Of more than one kind.
> Some come from ahead
> And some come from behind.[25]

Despite the fact that Geisel thought "I'm General Genghis

Kahn Schmitz" was a great line, the book was too bleak. Geisel biographers Judith and Neil Morgan called it "a Seussian *Pilgrim's Progress*."[26] The moral clearly was: *there are some troubles you can't avoid; there are some troubles you must face*. But the real lesson was: this book was chronically far too old for Dr. Seuss's typical child-readers and the message was something they couldn't really grasp (or didn't want to know) at their reading level.

Many Dr. Seuss books are near their hundredth re-printing: in 1997, *Solla Sollew* is in its twenty-second reprinting.

It was followed by two Theo. LeSieg books, *I Wish I Had Duck Feet* (1965) and *Come Over to My House* (1966).

In May, 1966, Bennett Cerf sold Random House to the RCA Corporation, at a time when many publishing firms were being bought or merged into conglomerates. It was then thought that the synergy would benefit broadcast and print properties; such isn't really the case and some broadcast/print properties were later divorced. (Time Warner is an example. The synergy between the Time Inc. magazines and the Warner film empire has never met original expectations, although there is some cross-promotion of Warner films promoted in the Time Inc. magazines.)

Back in La Jolla, Ted Geisel counted up and discovered that his stock in Beginner Books (and thus stock in Random House) sold to RCA made him a multi-millionaire. Random House is now part of Advance Publications, Inc. (which also owns *The New Yorker* magazine and other properties). Advance Publications is, in turn, owned by the Newhouse family.

Then Chuck Jones entered the picture (again). Friends from World War Two days, Jones believed that Dr. Seuss material could, and should, be made into a cartoon special for television. Typical negotiations followed, via Geisel's agents, potential sponsors, the Geisels and assorted friends and others.

It was early in 1966 and the calendar made the choice: by the end of the year Jones could have *The Grinch* ready for holiday viewing.

Jones moved The Grinch to animation without using any of the slapdash techniques of the time. Typical cartoons then used abbreviated action—backgrounds repeated (the same trees would reappear behind running figures, for instance) and voices didn't quite match actions. Jones used full-action techniques: 25,000 drawings instead of a typical cartoons 2,000 drawings.

The Grinch had to be reinvented. Colors—which colors should be used? What kind of a voice? How would the Whos be animated? and the length?—typically the Grinch story could be read aloud to an audience in less than 15 minutes. It had to be lengthened to almost a half-hour (minus time for commercials). Would the plot have to be changed, or added to?

Geisel wanted the Grinch to be in black-and-white—but Jones suggested that his eyes be a jealous green.

A Grinch song was added:

> You're a mean one, Mister Grinch;
> You really are a heel.
> You're as cuddly as a cactus, you're as charming as an eel.
> Mister Grinch! You're a bad banana
> with a greasy black peel . . . [27]

And, eventually, narrating the story was—the man with the perfect Grincy-y voice—Boris Karloff.

CBS-TV bought Grinch paying MGM $315,000 for two annual showings in 1966 and 1967. Chuck Jones predicted that it would be rerun "for at least the next ten years."[28]

He was wrong—*How the Grinch Stole Christmas!* has become an annual holiday event, along with Dickens' *A Christmas Carol* and another cartoon classic, *Charlie Brown's Christmas*, by Charles Schultz. Some things should just go on forever. *How The Grinch Stole Christmas!* is one—a holiday story with an obvious holiday moral, without being preachy or overly religious. In other words, perfect for everyone.

Chuck Jones then turned to animating *Horton Hears a Who!* with nearly the same results, except for the lack of seasonal fanfare. And Geisel turned to *The Cat in the Hat Songbook*, which he thought would be a natural for Cub Scout packs, Brownie troops, day care centers, communities, family sing-alongs. But the lyrics didn't match the melodies and the songs proved hard to sing. And *The Cat in the Hat Songbook* was the only other Dr. Seuss title beside *The Seven Lady Godivas* to be allowed to go out-of-print.

The Geisel's work continued. Helen Geisel worked with Beginner Books, with other projects of her own, with Ted and his new projects.

But on the morning of October 23, 1967, the housekeeper entered the Geisel's home and discovered that no one was up. Helen and Ted slept in separate bedrooms—and Ted was often late to bed and late to rise. That in itself was not unusual. But Helen was not up. The housekeeper, Alberta Shaw, found her in her bedroom.

Sometime during the night Helen Geisel, in constant pain since her first onset of Guillain-Barre syndrome and weakened by her bout with polio had taken her own life. She had overdosed with sodium pentobarbital tablets.

The woman who met Ted Geisel for the first time at Oxford, all those many years ago, who had picked him up, by looking over his shoulder while he was doodling, with the line, "say, that's a fine flying cow"—had taken her own life.

Although she had looked fine during the immediate past weeks, her mental condition had declined. No one knows how much physical pain she endured. She had left a note to Ted, surely as mixed a suicide note as there ever was.

> I feel myself in a spiral, going down down down, into a black hole from which there is no escape, no brightness. And loud in my ears from every side, I hear, "failure, failure, failure. . . ."

> I love you so much. . . . I am too old and enmeshed in everything you do and are, that I can not conceive of life without you. . . . My going will leave quite a rumor but you can say I was overworked and overwrought. Your reputation with your friends and fans will not be harmed. . . . Sometimes, think of the fun we had all thru the years. . . . ."[29]

Theodor Geisel was always fond of the mystical Seussian creatures which he created with such love and such abandon. And he was fond of fanciful names and mythical organizations. Helen Geisel signed her suicide note to Ted with the name of the law firm he created (and said he employed): Grimalkin, Drouberhannus, Knalbner and Fepp.

> *And I learned there are troubles of more than one kind.*
> *Some come from ahead and some come from behind. . . .*

Her obituary was run in the La Jolla/San Diego newspapers, in all the major California newspapers and, indeed, throughout the country, carried by the national wire services.

As he had done with the death of his sister, Marnie, Theodor Geisel bore his wife Helen's death in stoic silence; her part of the Dr. Seuss legacy was apportioned as she wished. The La Jolla Museum's Art-Reference Library was renamed the Helen Palmer Geisel Library; her share of some of the Dr. Seuss royalties went to Dartmouth for the Helen and Ted Geisel Third Century Professorship and other royalties and income went into the nonprofit Seuss Foundation. It was considerable.

Theodor Geisel was determined to stay in La Jolla, living as he had—as they had—on their mountaintop, where he had the views of the Pacific, La Jolla and San Diego, of much of California and parts of Mexico. He could look down on the beaches and the ocean surf, where he knew retired citizens of La Jolla had yachts in the water; retirement was not for him—certainly not at this moment.

Ted Geisel carried the grief of Helen's passing into his work. And working on additional books was the center of his life. It *was* his life.

He worked on another project—*The Foot Book*: this would not be a Beginner Books, but rather the first of the Bright and Early Books, whose reading level would pre-date Beginner Books. Ted Geisel believed that there was no time too early to read to children. He even believed that children should be read to in the womb, a notion which many pediatricians accepted as legitimate.

The Foot Book looks remarkably simplistic; for Geisel, the work was hard, made manifestly harder still by Helen's death. Catching the right rhyme and illustrating it appropriately was real work, hard work. Theodor Geisel usually put in eight-hour days when he was at work on a book, ignoring the ocean view to concentrate on the words in his head.

> Left foot
> Left foot
>
> Right foot
> Right

And, as usual, the illustrations marched toward the right, so little ones could follow toward the next page;

> Front feet
> Back feet
> Red feet
> Black feet[30]

The Foot Book was published in 1968 and no one reading it then (or today) could have guessed the tragedy involved during the months prior to its publication. Following the relative failure of *Solla Sollew*, *The Foot Book* marches on; as of mid-1997, it is in its 52nd reprinting and Bright and Early Books have proved as successful as Beginner Books.

And, in the same year, Theo. LeSieg published *The Eye Book*, illustrated by Roy McKie. It carried much the same page-by-page work scheme as *The Foot Book*. It was also a Bright and Early Book.

And Theodor Geisel's life changed, for the better, as do many whose spouses die unexpectedly. Into his life came Audrey Dimond, a La Jolla friend, who had known both Ted and Helen Geisel. She had been married to Grey Dimond, a cardiologist. Judith and Neil Morgan, in their biography, *Dr. Seuss and Mr. Geisel*, reprint this remarkable exchange between Grey and Audrey Dimond:

> . . . Audrey had approached her husband, Grey, in the kitchen of their Ludington Lane house to say that she planned to marry Ted. She realized that "something was lacking" in their marriage; she considered Grey self-sufficient, she told him, "but Ted needs me." The cardiologist had stood silently for a moment as though he were thinking all this over.
>
> "Who," he said finally, "is going to do the driving?"
>
> "Why, I guess, I will," Audrey replied, astonished.
>
> "Good," he said, "I don't want any wife of mine marrying a man who drives the way Ted does."[31]

In June, 1968, Ted Geisel and Audrey Dimond moved to Reno, into the Ponderosa Hotel, for the Nevada-required six-week waiting period to get married.

Theodor Geisel and Audrey Dimond were married quietly in Reno August 5, 1968.

At the end of the year, Geisel found himself in a legal battle over decades old Dr. Seuss material. He learned that the Universal Publishing Co., in New York, had contracted to reprint Dr. Seuss material from *Liberty* magazine, from about 1932. He spent

$100,000 in legal fees; the case went to U.S. District Judge William B. Herland in New York in December, but he ruled that Geisel had sold the material to *Liberty* at $300. per page. *Liberty* had the legal right to re-sell the material to Universal Publishing Co. The book, *Dr. Seuss' Lost World Revisited: A Forward-Looking Backward Glance* was published, but few Seuss enthusiasts have ever seen it. It exists now only in some library special collection departments.[32] Geisel needn't have spent his $100,000 on legal fees. It did nothing to damage his reputation.

Geisel was frequently at odds with contributors who could not live up to his exact standards for Beginner Books. He was particularly frustrated with Mike Frith, who worked with him on *My Book About Me*, an ingenious fill-in-the-blank book, in which the little owner was encouraged to past her or his photo on the front cover of the book and write inside, weight, number of teeth, address, an outline of the child's hand, and foot and on and on. On the inside left front cover is a space for the child's name (and a typical Seussian retort):

My Name is

____

I don't care
if you like
my name or not.
That's my name.
It's the only
name I've got.

Frith actually wanted to take a day off to watch Joe Namath and the New York Jets in Super Bowl III. Geisel was outraged that this heresy and carried his rage to Random House, where they all (including Robert Bernstein, who bore the brunt of his anger) were then astonished at *his* outrage.

So Geisel plotted. . . .

Carolyn See tells the story in "Dr. Seuss and the Naked Ladies," published in *Esquire*:

> In March of 1968, a scant month after Philip Roth had published *Portnoy's Complaint*, Theodor Seuss Geisel, the celebrated "Dr. Seuss," creator of grinches and hippografs, foxes in socks and cats in hats, wrote a five-page outline for a dirty book. He sent it to Robert Bernstein, successor to Bennett Cerf, and Seuss's own editor at Random House. Bernstein blanched, it is to be supposed, made emergency phone calls and called emergency meetings, all to discuss this more than dangerous aberration to which one of their leading, and certainly most wholesome, writers had succumbed. Dr. Seuss stayed home, meanwhile, didn't answer the phone and laughed himself sick.
>
> "I finally called Bernstein, after a week, and let him off the hook. He'd caught on by that time anyway."[33]

Interested fans often asked where he got his inspiration for the exotic locales and names in the Dr. Seuss books. Ted Geisel had been a world traveler with Helen Geisel. He and Helen had seen Europe and such areas as Peru, Turkey and the Yucatan region of Mexico; now he and Audrey traveled together. In the fall of 1969, they left California for Hawaii, then to Cambodia for visits to Angkor Watt, to India to see the Taj Mahal, to Tehran, to Jerusalem, where he was made an "Honorary Jew," by Teddy Kolleck, mayor of Jerusalem, then to Paris, then to London and then to New York, just in time for the release of *I Can Lick 30 Tigers Today! And Other Stories.*

(It seems logical, in retrospect, that Dr. Seuss obtained considerable inspiration for the strange locales and equally strange names he created, by visiting Peru, Turkey, the Yucatan, Angkor Watt, the Taj Mahal and on and on and on. These visits should almost be income-tax deductible expenses for Geisel, for the ideas, sketches and schemes he derived from seeing those exotic places. Other writers, not bankrolled by the very substantial royalties flowing from the Dr. Seuss sales, aren't quite lucky enough to travel so extensively.)

He next began *I Can Draw It Myself* , which he called "A revolt against coloring books," and *Mr. Brown Can Moo! Can You?*

In the past, Dr. Seuss had championed equality in *Horton Hears a Who!* and against Fascism/Nazism in "Yertle the Turtle" and against anti-semitism in "The Sneetches" (even though his child-readers may not understand the morals in "Yertle the Turtle" and "The Sneetches").

His pristine views from the top of Mount Soledad, he saw, were beginning to be spoiled by urban sprawl, apartments, condominiums, too much and too many, and that jolted him into action on a greater scale than *Mr. Brown Can Moo! Can You?*

But as much as he wanted to contribute something to what he saw as serious environmental damage, he didn't have a plot, characters or setting.

So he and Audrey decamped to Kenya, in September, 1970.

As typical tourists, they visited the common markets in Nairobi, then went to the Mt. Kenya Safari Club.

Years earlier, Dr. Seuss saw inspiration when a drawing of an elephant blew over a drawing of a tree. "What could an elephant be doing in a tree?" he asked and *Horton Hatches the Egg!* was born.

At the Mount Kenya Safari Club, Theodor Geisel was sitting and looking one afternoon, when a herd of elephants passed across the horizon, in front of the mountains.

Dr. Seuss was galvanized into furious work.

> I don't know what happened . . . I had nothing but a laundry list with me and I grabbed it . . . I wrote ninety percent of the book that afternoon. I got some kind of release watching those elephants

he later said.[34]

The book became one of his most controversial: *The Lorax.*

He took home photographs of the trees in the Serenghetti, which later became his silk-tufted Truffula trees.

He worked and worked on The Lorax, who "speaks for the trees." Eventually, The Lorax was short, old, brown and had a yellow bushy beard.

(To me, he looks like an animal cousin of Old Sneelock, in *If I Ran the Circus. . . .*)

> What was the Lorax?
> And why was it there?
> And why was it lifted and taken somewhere
> from the far end of town where the Grickle-grass grows?
> The old Once-ler still lives here.
> Ask him. *He* knows.
>
> You won't see the Once-ler.
> Don't knock at his door.

The Lorax begins at night, with dark shades of blues, greens, taupes—and the Once-ler is never completely seen—only his eyes, green arms and green hands.

Like the Ancient Mariner, the Once-ler tells *his* ancient story—but only after you pay him: The Once-ler's story is one of greed, pure and simple. The Truffula Trees had all been cut down for garments called Thneeds.

A Thneed was an all-purpose garment which everybody could wear and everybody could need. But a Lorax popped out of the cut stump and warned against spoiling the forests.

The Once-ler built a whole factory and cut down all the Truffula Trees, to make Thneeds, which everyone needs.

The Lorax warned about losing all the forests.

Children who are too young to understand equality, and surely too young to understand the perils of Fascism and Nazism and 'way too young to understand why some Sneetches wear stars and some have no stars . . . these readers could surely see the poor Brown Barba-loots which looked like Seussian brown bears, waving sadly, as they walked away from their ruined forest.

And we can almost hear some little girl or boy, talking to the pictures: *Goodbye, Bar-ba-loots, Goodbye. . . .*

But the Once-ler's factory worked overtime, making Thneeds which everyone needs and the sky became grey and the Swomee-Swans can no longer sing for the smog in their throats.

And there was pollution in the ponds, too.

And then the Once-ler cut down the very last Truffula Tree.

And the Lorax left, uttering one word: *Unless*.[35]

> The master of nonsense turning his deft pen to such serious subjects as ecological disaster? Nonsense. Yet Dr. Seuss' (book) happens to be very good indeed (though not really vintage Seussiana),

said *The Christian Science Monitor*.[36]

And *Library Journal* wrote,

> The big colorful pictures in Dr. Seuss's typically lively, cartoonish style, and the fun images, word plays and rhymes make this an amusing, if unsubtle, exposition of the ecology crisis.[37]

The Lorax would always be considered his most controversial book.[38]

Seven

1971–1991

Oh, the places you'll go . . .

Before *The Lorax* was published, Ted Geisel had met Liz Carpenter, Secretary to Ladybird Johnson, and during a pleasant conversation, he told her about *The Lorax*. She suggested because of the environmental nature of the book, it would surely help Ladybird Johnson's campaign in cleaning up the environment. Would Geisel consider contributing the manuscript to the Lyndon Johnson Presidential Library in Austin, Texas? So Geisel called Lyndon Johnson at the LBJ Ranch in the Hill Country of Texas. Would the President like to have the manuscript and art for *The Lorax*? The President would indeed, so the Geisels journeyed to Austin to present *The Lorax* materials to the LBJ Library personally.

That was a plus.

Just several years later, Dr. Seuss helped bring down a president.

He had completed a Bright and Early book, *Marvin K. Mooney, Will You Please Go Now!*, in 1972, about a rascal of a kid who wouldn't go home. Dr. Seuss wrote:

> The
>
> time
>
> has come.

The time has come.
The time is now.
Just go.
Go.
GO![1]

But Marvin K. Mooney won't leave.

Ted Geisel had previously met Art Buchwald and they had become good friends. When Buchwald published *I Never Danced at the White House*, he sent Geisel a copy and dared Geisel to write a political book.

Theodor Geisel did it faster than Buckwald ever expected.

It was then July, 1974, and the Watergate investigation was juggernauting toward its inevitable conclusion. Theodor Geisel took a copy of *Marvin K. Mooney . . .*

And revised throughout the book:

The time has come.
The time has come.
The time is now.

Just go.
Go.
GO! I don't care how.

You can go by foot.
You can go by cow.
Richard M. Nixon,
will you please go now!

. . . and sent the book to Art Buchwald. Geisel told Random House what he had done with one copy of *Marvin K. Mooney . . .* and "they went nuts," in his words. But he gave Buchwald permission to use it.

Buchwald ran the book, with Dr. Seuss's revisions, in his nationwide column.

And nine days later . . .

> The time had come.
> SO . . .
> Nixon WENT.[2]

Buchwald claimed the credit and Dr. Seuss was a willing accomplice.

Also in 1972, *The Lorax* was made into a cartoon, like *How The Grinch Stole Christmas! The Lorax* was narrated by actor Eddie Albert and it too, was a success.

For 13 years following the publication of *The Lorax*, in 1971, Theodor Geisel worked on an annual release of one or more Beginner Books or Bright and Early books. (Those he published under the pseudonym Theo. LeSieg were books which were smaller in format than the Dr. Seuss books—for either of the two series—and the LeSieg books were written by Geisel but illustrated by Seuss and others.) They were:

* *In A People House*, 1972;
* *Marvin K. Mooney, Will You Please Go Now!*, 1972;
* *The Many Mice of Mr. Brice*, 1973;
* *Did I Ever Tell You How Lucky You Are?*, 1973;
* *The Shape of Me and Other Stuff*, 1973;
* *Great Day for Up!*, 1974;
* *There's a Wocket in My Pocket!*, 1974 in which he writes:

> Did you
> ever have the feeling
> there's a
> WASKET
> in your
> BASKET?

. . . Or a NUREAU
in your BUREAU?[3]

Here was Theodor Geisel again being subversive; teaching children sounds with nonsense stories . . .

* *Wacky Wednesday,* 1974;
* *Because a Little Bug Went Ka-Choo!*, 1974, and for that book he worked closely with Michael Firth. Because they worked so closely together, the book was hardly just a Theo. LeSieg book. Audrey Geisel walked into the studio during a time when they were thinking of a pseudonym; Firth suggest that they name it after her. Geisel said her maiden name was Stone; instantly the pseudonym became Rosetta Stone.
* *Oh, the Thinks You Can Think!*, 1974;
* *Would You Rather Be a Bullfrog?*, 1975;
* *Hooper Humperdink. . . ? Not Him!*, 1975;
* *The Cat's Quizzer,* 1976;
* *Try to Remember the First of Octember,* 1977;
* *I Can Read With My Eyes Shut!*, 1978;
* *Oh Say Can You Say?*, 1979;
* *Maybe You Should Fly a Jet! Maybe You Should Be a Vet!*, 1980;
* *The Tooth Book,* 1981;
* *Hunches in Bunches,* 1982.

His readers would never know that, in the mid-1970s, Dr. Seuss and Theo. LeSieg were getting older. Ted Geisel discovered one morning in 1975 that he couldn't see. Momentarily panicking, he called Audrey, who in turned called in an eye specialist. She feared cataracts; the specialists diagnosed cataracts *and* glaucoma. For five years, Geisel endured operations for both cataracts and glaucoma. Some days he could see with his left eye perfectly but his right eye was still damaged. He compensated by making his storyboards larger than normal; when they were shipped to Random House, they were reduced to regular page size.

Surely, his eye problems contributed to the 1978 book, *I Can Read With My Eyes Shut!* although again, young readers couldn't have realized that either. It took five years for the eye problems to be resolved and his sight restored.

In June of 1977, Theodor Geisel was awarded an honorary degree at Lake Forest College, near Chicago. His commencement address took less than two minutes to read; and in an age when 98 and 3/4ths percent of all commencement addresses are forgettable as soon as the graduates and happy parents have left the coliseum, no one could forget this bit of wisdom from Dr. Seuss:

My Uncle Terwilliger on the Art of Eating Popovers

My uncle ordered popovers
from the restaurant's bill of fare.
And when they were served,
he regarded them
with a penetrating stare . . .
Then he spoke great Words of Wisdom
as he sat there on that chair:
"To eat these things,"
said my uncle,
"You must exercise great care.
You may swallow down what's solid . . .
BUT . . .
you *must* spit out the air!"

And . . .
as *you* partake of the world's bill of fare,
that's darn good advise to follow.
Do a lot of spitting out the hot air.
And be careful what you swallow.

* * *

Age again crept closer to Dr. Seuss and to Ted Geisel. Although his eye problems had been cleared up, in 1981, he suffered from "indigestion" one day then again the next day and then Audrey took him to the hospital where the diagnosis was that he had suffered a heart attack; relatively small, but a heart attack nonetheless.[5] He had been a chain-smoker but reluctantly gave it up—he found a pipe that he hadn't used for years—decades earlier, really—and filled it with radish seeds. Occasionally, when he was thinking Big Thinks, he would water the pipe with an eyedropper. And when he had forgotten what was in his pipe, radish greens grew out of the bowl.

Age continued to creep closer.

During a dental exam, a lesion was discovered at the base of his tongue; cancerous and potentially very dangerous, Geisel submitted to a procedure that placed an implant under his tongue to neutralize the cancer.

Out of the hospital, Geisel marveled at the Reagan administration's vision of a potential nuclear war with Russia. And then he remembered—or seemed to recall from his European days years earlier, the Guelphs and the Ghibellines of the north of Italy, who fought a war because one side favored the Pope and the other side was anti-Pope. Or, rather, Dr. Seuss remembered them because one side cut their apples vertically and the other side cut their apples horizontally. That was Seussian history, as he recalled it.

Thus was born his second-most-controversial book, *The Butter Battle Book*, Dr. Seuss's statement on the futility of war: about the competing tribes, the Zooks and the Yooks.

And, of course, the Zooks watched the Yooks, and one of the Zooks fired a slingshot at a Yook . . . who got together with a council of Yooks, and made a monstrous triple-threat slingshot . . . and the Zooks replied with a triple-threat slingshot catcher . . . and then the Yooks . . ."carefully trained a real smart dog named Daniel to serve as our country's first gun-toting spaniel."[6]

But the other side invented an Eight-Nozzled, Elephant-Toted Boom-Blitz . . . and . . . a Big Boy Boomeroo . . . of a weapon.

Both sides eventually had bands, and cheerleaders and uniforms and flying machines and bombs . . . for war.

And Dr. Seuss leaves the conclusion hanging on edge:

> "Grandpa," I shouted, "Be careful! Oh, gee!
> Who's going to drop it?
> Will *you*. . . ? Or will *he*. . . ?
> "Be patient," said Grandpa, "We'll see.
> We will see . . ."[7]

When he took the book to Random House, he said "I have no idea if this is an adult book for children or a children's book for adults . . ." and said he always wanted to write a "lady and the tiger" ending.[8]

He and Random House people went 'round and 'round, like the Gingham Dog and the Calico Cat, about the title and the cover and the ending and the message . . . were children old enough to understand war for seemingly trivial principles?

Janet Schulman, editor in chief, sent proofs to children's author Maurice Sendak, who returned the definitive blurb about *The Butter Battle Book*:

> Surprisingly, wonderfully, the case for total disarmament has been brilliantly made by our acknowledged master of nonsense, Dr. Seuss . . . Only a genius of the ridiculous could possibly deal with the cosmic and lethal madness of the nuclear arms race . . . He has done the world a service.[9]

The message was not used on the cover, but it was enough. *The Butter Battle Book* went to press with the cover as Dr. Seuss drew it and with the message that Dr. Seuss had intended.

The Big Boy Boomeroo of age inched closer. In December,

1983, Theodor Geisel had an operation and a deep biopsy of the area of his neck where the lesion was first spotted. His neck was disfigured, but the operation was a necessity to stop any further spread of cancer.

But, as Random House people first thought, *The Butter Battle Book* was received critically with strong reservations:

> The language of the story rhymes and amuses in customary Seuss fashion, and the colorful cartoon drawings are zesty and humorous. Seuss is in a category of his own in both originality and popularity, and the demand for this book will undoubtedly be large. One wonders, however, if a book for young children is a suitable vehicle for such an accurate and uncloaked description of the current stalemate in nuclear arms disarmament. . . . This story ends without the slightest glimmer of hope that a solution to the standoff will be found, and as such can only contribute to a child's sense of helplessness. On this issue, perhaps above all others, it is critical to communicate to children the possibility of finding solutions beyond those immediately visible.
>
> —Anne L. Okie, *School Library Journal*[10]

> "(This) is probably the most thinly veiled allegory Geisel has written. It's not a funny book. Clearly, he feels seriously about the arms race. . . . To some persons, "The Butter Battle Book" may not seem like ideal children's fare. The book depends heavily on the implicit urgency of the arms control issue. We all know it is important (so the argument goes) and therefore our children should know about it. But should they? What Geisel rather disparagingly calls "a happy ending" may in fact be the ray of hope that children need when learning about adult troubles. It is not fashionable to be optimistic about the nuclear arms race. But, if the future of the world rests

> with children, shouldn't they learn that, in addition to seeing evil, mankind is capable of averting it as well?
>
> —Gloria Goodale, *The Christian Science Monitor*[11]

The world survived the nuclear arms race, children everywhere survived Dr. Seuss's moralizing and *The Butter Battle Book* is still in print.

When the book was released, Random House officials, including Donald and Samuel Newhouse (Random House was now owned by the Newhouse family, through their Advance Publications Company), took him to luncheon at New York's "21" club. It was fifty years since Bennett Cerf took him to lunch and took him into the Random House family from Vanguard Press. Bennett Cerf had since died, but Dr. Seuss and Random House continued on. . . .

Dr. Seuss was pleased that right after *The Butter Battle Book* was shown on television in the Soviet Union on New Years Day of 1990, the U.S.S.R. began to fall apart. Since he and Art Buchwald caused the downfall of the Nixon administration with "Richard M. Nixon, will you please go now!" it was only right that Dr. Seuss by himself caused the downfall of the giant Potemkin village that was the Soviet Empire.

And then Dr. Seuss won the Pulitzer Prize. Ted Geisel was astonished. The Pulitzer was "usually given to adults. I'm a writer who had to eat with the children before the adults eat," he said.[13]

Clearly now he was at the head of the table; at about that time, Dr. Seuss books were being published in over 20 languages and the baby-boom generation guaranteed sales that multiplied phenomenally, book after book, year after year.

Audrey tricked him into going to Princeton University in the spring of 1985; he discovered that Princeton would be awarding him an honorary doctorate. When he got up to walk to receive his diploma, in a move that can't be imagined for any other writer, the entire graduating class rose, chanted the full book-length text of *Green Eggs and Ham*.[14]

Back in La Jolla, Geisel considered all his recent illness, operations, for his eyes, which resulted in *I Can Read With My Eyes Shut!* and his recent operation for the cancer in his throat. He retold his latest encounters with doctors and hospitals in another book and that, perhaps more than any therapy or treatment was good for him. For the first time since *The Seven Lady Godivas*, he was not writing a book for children. Ted Geisel had always said, "adults are only obsolete children and to hell with 'em." On the front cover is the subtitle:

A Book for Obsolete Children

The book was *You're Only Old Once!*:

Just why are you here?
Not feeling your best . . .

You've come in for
An Eyesight and Solvency Test.

And here Dr. Seuss shows a progressively larger eye chart which reads:

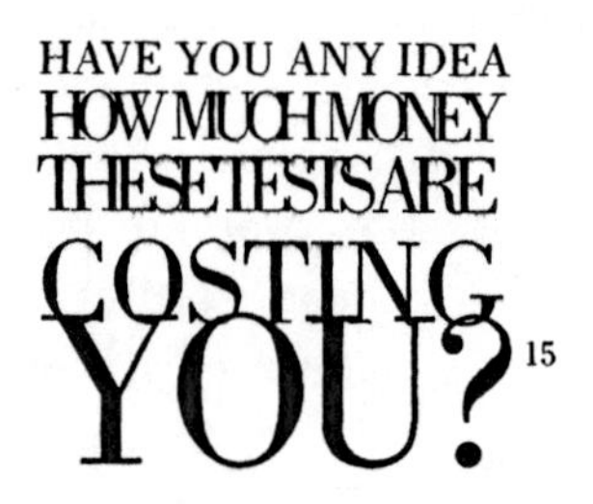

[15]

He is battered by every test imaginable, for every specialty known to science.

Ultimately, after all the testing and poking and prodding (and billing), the best doctor of all, Dr. Seuss, offers a positive diagnosis:

> you're in pretty good shape
> for the shape you are in![16]

And indeed, he was in pretty good shape for the shape he was in: the book was written and published when he was 82. Random House publishing panjandrums had worried that the book would not sell—it clearly wasn't a book for the usual audience for Dr. Seuss books: children. And would adults buy it? Adults really didn't read Dr. Seuss books, unless the Seuss books were thrust at them by small hands to be read at bedtime.

Dr. Seuss was righter than right. As usual. The first printing of 200,000 copies sold out and the book had to go back to press. Early Dr. Seuss children had, by now, become adults (and had children of and perhaps grandchildren of their own). So the "obsolete children" bought this book for themselves and savored the pictures they saw in the book—of themselves getting older.

The book sold and sold. It hit the number one spot on *The New York Times* best-seller list; after five months it had sold 600,000 copies and by the end of the first year had sold one million copies and was in its ninth printing.[17]

Dr. Seuss was much more than a best-selling author; he was a cultural icon. A retrospective collection of his work was displayed in the San Diego Museum and drew huge crowds, although the art critic of the *San Diego Union* panned it as not a collection about *art*. That shows toured the country, stopping at various museums: the Carnegie Museum of Art in Pittsburgh; the Baltimore Museum of Art; the New Orleans Museum of Art and the Queens Museum of Art in New York.

He and Helen toured his hometown of Springfield, Massachusetts, some twenty years after the death of Geisel's father.

They walked along Mulberry Street and the Mayor gave him a metal outdoor sign, *Geisel Grove*, found in the park that Geisel's father had so carefully nurtured. Later on Mulberry Street, sightseeing in an antique bus, Geisel was startled to see two hundred school children appear, holding a huge sign:

AND TO THINK THAT I SAW HIM ON
MULBERRY STREET!

Geisel was speechless with tears.[18] And although the situations changed from locale to locale, that spirit was how he was received anywhere he made a public appearance.

But the Big Boomeroo of age and health was still closing in. By 1985 he had weakened. The cancer in his throat had been halted, but the by-product of the cancer treatments was an infection in his jaw, impossible to eradicate. And he was increasingly infirm, with bouts of gout and loss of hearing typical of advancing age, and more and more turned down invitations for social events, especially outside La Jolla.

Projects didn't jell; there was no Horton blown onto an elephant as an idea to seize on. He began books, abandoned them—the outside world saw him as an exalted figure; in his studio, nothing seemed to work.

Except . . . the cynical dictum from his Dartmouth years:

Oh, the places you'll go . . .

That worked: the cynical phrase from his callow college days was the key to another Dr. Seuss book. How graduation, from either high school or college is a pretty scary thing. Stepping into the dark, walking who-knows-where . . . taking tentative steps into the dark of a big world:

> Congratulations!
> Today is your day.

You're off to Great Places
You're off and away!

You have brains in your head.
You have feet in your shoes.
You can steer yourself
any direction you choose . . . [19]

You're on your own, and you know what you know.
And *YOU* are the guy who'll decide where to go.

It was Dr. Seuss's last book; when he was working on it, he seemed to know that, and so did those around him.

He knew his audience, just like he had known the audience for *You're Only Old Once! Oh, The Places You'll Go!* hit the top of *The New York Times* best-seller lists and stayed there for more than two years. During that time, it sold one and one-half million copies![20]

But while waiting for *The Places You'll Go!* to appear, Audrey Geisel felt herself sinking, sinking into some vague illness, something that she thought might be Alzheimer's. She finally got a diagnosis and discovered that a tumor was pushing against her brain. An operation was successful and she was on her way again.

He read an essay in *The New York Review of Books*, by novelist Alison Lurie, which charged him with sexism. All the main characters in his books, were little boys, she claimed. Geisel believed that most of the characters in his books were animals and "if she could identify their sex, I'll remember her in my will," but in *Daisy-Head Mayzie*, published posthumously, for the first time in a Seuss book, the hero is a little girl.

Slowly, bit by bit, Dr. Seuss put his work away; there was no agony, no pain. He began sleeping on a sofa in his studio. Once, when Audrey awakened him, he asked, plaintively, "am I dead yet?"[23]

In the evening of September 24, 1991, Dr. Seuss died peacefully in his sleep, in his mountaintop studio in La Jolla.

Years earlier, Helen Geisel had to undergo a sudden, traumatic (and unexplained) operation. He never had any children of his own. But in fact, the children of the country and the whole world were his.

He loved them and they loved him.

And they love him still.

Epilogue

"... to a unique and hallowed place *in the nurseries* of the world ..."

All of the Random House Dr. Seuss books, except for *The Seven Lady Godivas* and *The Cat in the Hat Songbook* remain in print and, following his death, there have also been additional Dr. Seuss books published.

Daisy-Head Mayzie was published in 1995 as was *The Secret Art of Dr. Seuss*, abstract paintings with fanciful names, which were art works unrelated to any of his books. *My Many Colored Days*, with illustrations by Steve Johnson and Lou Fancher and an anthology, *A Hatful of Seuss*, containing *If I Ran the Zoo*; *The Sneetches and Other Stories; Horton Hears a Who!; Dr. Seuss's Sleep Book* and *Bartholomew and the Oobleck* were also published in 1996.

Seuss-isms: Wise and Witty Prescriptions for Living from the Good Doctor, a "stocking-stuffer"-sized book of aphorisms was published in 1997.

Horray for Diffendoofer Day has been published in 1998; it was based on notes Geisel left uncompleted in his study during his lifetime; it was eventually written by Jack Prelutsky and the art was supplied by Lane Smith.

There is now a "second generation" of Seuss material. His widow and literary agents have licensed the Dr. Seuss name to the Jim Henson Studios and they have created *The Wubbulous World of Dr. Seuss*, a television cartoon series for children. And that television series has resulted in spin-off books also published by Random House.

Theodor Geisel by himself, created a revolution in children's books. He single-handedly eliminated the "See Dick, See Jane, See Spot," readers from millions of classrooms and libraries—simplistic books which had bored children for decades.

His books challenged children to use their imaginations; he took them to imaginary locales aboard fantastical animals and taught them lessons about equality, the environment, duty ("I meant what I said and I said what I meant, an elephant's faithful, one hundred percent . . .") and the true value of Christmas . . .

In the words of a young boy, referring to Seuss, "you have an imagination with a long tail . . ."

By the 1970s he had become an icon. In 1999, the Postal Service issued a Cat in the Hat U.S. stamp.

Interviewed by Hilliard Harper in *The Los Angeles Times Magazine* in 1986,[1] Geisel said,

> I think I had something to do with kicking Dick and Jane out of the school system. I think I proved to a number of million kids that reading is not a disagreeable task. And without talking about teaching, I think I have helped kids laugh in schools as well as home. That's about enough, isn't it?

After his death, *Time* magazine headlined his obituary "The Doctor Beloved By All"[2]:

> He was one of the last doctors to make house calls—some 200 million of them in 20 languages. By the time of his death last week at 87, Dr. Seuss had journeyed on beyond Dr. Spock to a unique and hallowed place in the nurseries of the world.

Bibliography

Books by Theodor "Dr. Seuss" Geisel

1937: *And To Think That I Saw It on Mulberry Street.* New York: The Vanguard Press.

1938: *The 500 Hats of Bartholomew Cubbins.* New York: The Vanguard Press.

1939: *The Seven Lady Godivas.* New York: Random House.

1940: *Horton Hatches the Egg.* New York: Random House.

1947: *McElligot's Pool.* New York: Random House.

1948: *Thidwick the Big-Hearted Moose.* New York: Random House.

1949: *Bartholomew and the Oobleck.* New York: Random House.

1950: *If I Ran the Zoo.* New York: Random House.

1953: *Scrambled Eggs Super!* New York: Random House.

1954: *Horton Hears a Who!* New York: Random House.

1955: *On Beyond Zebra!* New York: Random House.

1956: *If I Ran the Circus.* New York: Random House.

1957: *How the Grinch Stole Christmas!* New York: Random House.

1957: *The Cat in the Hat.* New York: Random House.

1958: *The Cat in the Hat Comes Back.* New York: Random House.

1958: *Yertle the Turtle and Other Stories.* New York: Random House.

1959: *Happy Birthday to You!* New York: Random House.

1960: *Green Eggs and Ham.* New York: Random House.
1960: *One Fish Two Fish Red Fish Blue Fish.* New York: Random House.
1961: *The Sneetches and Other Stories.* New York: Random House.
1961: *Ten Apples Up on Top.* (Theo LeSieg, pseudonym). New York: Random House.
1962: *Dr. Seuss's Sleep Book.* New York: Random House.
1963: *Hop on Pop.* New York: Random House.
1963: *Dr. Seuss's ABC.* New York: Random House.
1965: *Fox in Sox.* New York: Random House.
1965: *I Had Trouble Getting to Solla Sollew.* New York: Random House.
1965: *I Wish I Had Duck Feet.* (Theo. LeSieg, pseudonym.) New York: Random House.
1966: *Come Over to My House.* (Theo., LeSieg, pseudonym.) New York: Random House.
1967: *The Cat in the Hat Song Book.* New York: Random House.
1968: *The Foot Book.* New York: Random House.
1968: *The Eye Book.* (Theo, LeSieg, pseudonym.) New York: Random House.
1968: *Dr. Seuss' Lost World Revisited: A Forward-Looking Backward Glance.* New York: Universal Publishing Co.
1969: *I Can Lick 50 Tigers Today! and Other Stories.* New York: Random House.
1969: *My Book About Me—By Me, Myself, I Wrote It! I Drew It!* New York: Random House.
1970: *I Can Draw It Myself.* New York: Random House.
1970: *Mr. Brown Can Moo! Can You?* New York: Random House.
1971: *I Can Write—by Me, Myself* (Theo. Leseig, pseudonym.) New York: Random House.
1971: *The Lorax.* New York: Random House.
1972: *In a People House.* (Theo. LeSieg, pseudonym.) New York: Random House.
1972: *Marvin K. Mooney, Will You Please Go Now!* New York: Random House.

1973: *The Many Mice of Mr. Bice.* (Theo. LeSieg, pseudonym.) New York: Random House.
1973: *Did I Ever Tell You How Lucky You Are?* New York: Random House.
1973: *The Shape of Me and Other Stuff.* New York: Random House.
1974: *Great Day for Up!* New York: Random House.
1974: *There's a Wocket in My Pocket!* New York: Random House.
1974: *Wacky Wednesday.* (Theo. LeSieg, pseudonym.) New York: Random House.
1975: *Because a Little Bug Went Ka-Choo!* (Rosetta Stone, pseudonym.) New York: Random House.
1975: *Oh, The Thinks You Can Think!* New York: Random House.
1975: *Would You Rather be a Bullfrog?* (Theo. LeSieg, pseudonym.) New York: Random House.
1976: *Hooper Humperdink. . . ? Not Him!* (Theo. LeSieg, pseudonym.) New York: Random House.
1976: *The Cat's Quizzer.* New York: Random House.
1977: *Try to Remember the First of Octember.* (Theo. LeSieg, pseudonym.) New York: Random House.
1978: *I Can Read with My Eyes Shut!* New York: Random House.
1979: *Oh Say Can You Say?* New York: Random House.
1980: *Maybe You Should Fly a Jet! Maybe You Should be a Vet!* (Theo. LeSieg, pseudonym.) New York: Random House.
1981: *The Tooth Book.* (Theo. LeSieg, pseudonym.) New York: Random House.
1982: *Hunches in Bunches.* New York: Random House.
1984: *The Butter Battle Book.* New York: Random House.
1986: *You're Only Young Once!* New York: Random House.
1987: *I'm Not Going to Get Up Today!* New York: Random House.
1990: *Oh! The Places You'll Go.* New York: Random House.
1991: *Six by Seuss: A Treasury of Dr. Seuss Classics.* New York: Random House.
1995: *Daisy-Head Mayzie.* New York: Random House.
1995: *The Secret Art of Dr. Seuss.* New York: Random House.

1996: *My Many-Colored Days.* New York: Alfred Knopf.
1996: *A Hatfull of Seuss.* New York: Random House.
1997: *Seuss-isms: Wise and Witty Prescriptions for Living from the Good Doctor.* New York: Random House.
1998: *Hooray for Diffendoofer Day.* New York: Random House.
1999: *Dr. Seuss Goes to War: The World War II Editorial Cartoons of Theodore Seuss Geisel.* New York: The Free Press.

Secondary Sources

Cerf, Bennett. *At Random: The Reminiscences of Bennett Cerf.* New York: Random House, 1977.

Cott, Jonathan. *Pipers at the Gate of Dawn: The Wisdom of Children's Literature.* New York: Random House, 1983.

Dr. Seuss From Then to Now. New York: Random House, 1986.

Fensch, Thomas, ed. *Of Sneetches and Whos and the Good Doctor Seuss: Essays on the Writings and Life of Theodor Geisel.* Jefferson, N.C.: McFarland & Co., 1997.

Hulbert, Dan. "SEUSS-travaganza." *Houston* (Tx.) *Chronicle*, Aug. 3, 2000, pp. D 1, D 4.

Lanes, Selma G. *Down the Rabbit Hole: Adventures and Misadventures in the Realm of Children's Literature.* New York: Atheneum, 1971.

MacDonald, Ruth K. *Dr. Seuss.* New York: Wayne Publishers, 1988.

Marschall, Richard, ed. *The Tough Coughs as He Plows the Dough: Early Writings and Cartoons by Dr. Seuss.* New York: William Morrow, 1987.

Minear, Richard H., ed. *Dr. Seuss Goes to War: The World War II Editorial Cartoons of Theodor Seuss Geisel.* New York: The Free Press, 1999.

Morgan, Judith and Morgan, Neil. *Dr. Seuss and Mr. Geisel.* New York: Random House, 1995.

Notes

Prologue

1) Wilder, Rob. "Catching Up With Dr. Seuss," *Parents* magazine, June, 1978, pp. 63.
2) Morgan, Judith and Morgan, Neil, *Dr. Seuss and Mr. Geisel*, pp. 6.
3) Ibid., pp. 18–19.
4) Ibid., pp. 34.

One

1) Morgan and Morgan, p. 3.
2) Ibid., pp. 5.
3) Ibid., pp. 6.
4) Ibid., pp. 6
5) Ibid., pp. 6–7.
6) Ibid., pp. 7. The pie poem was one of his earliest memories, but as far as is known, he never used it in any of his books.
7) Ibid., pp. 7.
8) Ibid., pp. 9.
9) Ibid., pp. 11–12.
10) Ibid., pp. 12
11) Ibid., pp. 13
12) Quoted in Morgan and Morgan, pp. 21.
13) Ibid., pp. 21–22.

14) Ibid., pp. 23
15) Edward Connery Lathem, "The Beginnings of Dr. Seuss: A Conversation with Theodor Geisel," *Dartmouth Alumni Magazine*, April, 1976.
16) Ibid.
17) *Hillaire Belloc's Cautionary Tales.* (Reprint ed. Gregg Press, div. of G. K. Hall & Co., Boston, 1979). No pagination.
18) Ibid., pp. 17–24.
19) Morgan and Morgan, pp. 25.
20) Martin Gardner. *The Annotated Alice.* (New York: Clarkson N. Potter Co., 1960). pp. 69–70.
21) Introduction, *Hillaire Belloc's Cautionary Tales*, no pagination.
22) Morgan and Morgan, pp. 28.
23) Ibid., pp. 30.
24) Ibid., pp. 28.
25) Lathem.
26) Morgan and Morgan, pp. 32.
27) Lathem.
28) Lathem.
29) Morgan and Morgan, pp. 33.
30) Ibid., pp. 34.
31) Ibid., pp. 35–36.
32) Ibid., pp. 36.
33) Lathem.
34) Morgan and Morgan, pp. 37.
35) Ibid., pp. 38.
36) Ibid., pp. 41.
37) Ibid., pp. 42.
38) Ibid., pp. 44–45.
39) Lathem.
40) Morgan and Morgan, pp. 45.
41) Lathem.
42) Lathem.
43) Morgan and Morgan, pp. 50.

44) Ibid., pp. 52.
45) Lathem.
46) Morgan and Morgan, pp. 54.
47) Mary Stofflet, in *Dr. Seuss from Then to Now*, pp. 21.
48) Lathem.
49) Morgan and Morgan, pp. 58.
50) Ibid., pp. 58. Boni and Liveright was a book publisher; Bennett Cerf would buy The Modern Library from Horace Liveright to establish Random House. *Judge*, the humor magazine would not long survive.
51) *Life* magazine, the humor magazine. Henry Luce would buy *Life*, kill it in its original form and use just the name for a new magazine he was developing—a picture magazine which his wife, Claire Booth Luce had, in part, suggested.
52) But like a man who wears both a belt and suspenders, under Seuss, the *Post* editors ran: "Drawn by Theodor Seuss Geisel." Morgan and Morgan, pp. 59.

Two

1) Morgan and Morgan, pp. 60–61.
2) Reprinted in Richard Marschall, *The Thought Coughs as he Ploughs the Dough: Early Writings and Cartoons by Dr. Seuss*, pp. 10.
3) Mary Stofflet, in *Dr. Seuss from Then to Now*, pp. 23.
4) Morgan and Morgan, pp. 62–63.
5) Lathem.
6) Morgan and Morgan, pp. 63.
7) Lathem.
8) Morgan and Morgan, pp. 65.
9) Lathem.
10) Lathem.
11) In Marschall, pp. 11.
12) Reprinted in Marschall, pp. 57.
13) Lathem.

14) Morgan and Morgan, pp. 71–72.
15) Ibid., pp. 72.
16) Stofflet, in *Dr. Seuss from Then to Now*, pp. 24–25.
17) Morgan and Morgan, pp. 74–75.
18) Jonathan Cott, *Pipers at the Gates of Dawn: The Wisdom of Children's Literature*, pp. 17.
19) Lathem.
20) *Dr. Seuss From Then to Now*, pp. 23.
21) Bob Warren, *The Dartmouth*, May 10, 1935, reprinted in Morgan and Morgan, pp. 76.
22) Morgan and Morgan, pp. 79.
23) The Moth-Watching Sneth and the Grickily Gractus are from *Scrambled Eggs Super!*—TF.
24) *The Horn Book* magazine, Sept. 1992.
25) Lathem.
26) Morgan and Morgan, pp. 80.
27) Ibid., pp. 82.
28) Selma G. Lanes, *Down the Rabbit Hole: Adventures* and *Misadventures in the Realm of Children's Literature*, pp. 79–80.
29) Cott, pp. 28.
30) Morgan and Morgan, pp. 83.
31) *The New Yorker*, pp. XXX.
32) *The New York Times*, Nov. 14, 1937.
33) *The Atlantic Monthly*, Nov., 1937.
34) Morgan and Morgan, pp. 84.
35) Peter Bunzel, "The Wacky World of Dr. Seuss," *Life*, April 5, 1959; also cited in Morgan and Morgan, pp. 85.
36) Morgan and Morgan, pp. 85.
37) Ibid.
38) *Dartmouth Alumni Magazine*, Jan. 1939, reprinted in Morgan and Morgan, pp. 88.
39) Bennett Cerf. *At Random*. (New York: Random House, 1977), pp. 27–57.
40) Ibid., pp. 65.
41) Ibid., pp. 93.

42) Ibid., pp. 105.
43) Ibid., pp. 153.
44) Stofflet, in *Dr. Seuss from Then to Now*, pp. 31.
45) Cerf, pp. 154.
46) In *Dr. Seuss from Then to Now*, pp. 27.
47) Lanes, pp. 88.
48) Like his purchase of the firm Smith and Hass, which enlarged Random House, Bennett Cerf eventually bought The Vanguard Press at least in part, to bring the first two Dr. Seuss books into Random House . . .

Three

1) Reprinted in Morgan and Morgan, pp. 96.
2) *The King's Stilts*, no pagination.
3) Ibid.
4) Cerf. *At Random*, pp. 153.
5) Morgan and Morgan, pp. 96.
6) Geisel, reprinted in Morgan and Morgan, pp. 97. Miller, Haas, Klopfer and Commins were all executives at Random House.
7) Ibid., pp. 97–98.
8) Dr. Seuss, *Horton Hatches the Egg!*, no pagination.
9) *The New York Times*, Oct. 13, 1940, pp. 10.
10) In Morgan and Morgan, pp. 103.
11) Ibid., pp. 104.
12) Ibid., pp. 101–102.
13) Helen Geisel, quoted in Morgan and Morgan, pp. 105.
14) In Morgan and Morgan, pp. 107.
15) Reprinted in Morgan and Morgan, pp. 111.
16) E.J. Kahn, Jr., "Children's Friend," *The New Yorker*, Dec. 17, 1960.
17) Morgan and Morgan, pp. 119–120.
18) Ibid., pp. 121.
19) Morgan and Morgan, pp. 121.
20) Oct. 18, 1947.

21) Oct. 1, 1947.
22) Nov. 15, 1947.
23) *Thidwick, The Big-Hearted Moose*, 1948, no pagination.
24) Nov. 14, 1948.
25) Oct. 10, 1948, pp. 25
26) Nov. 14, 1948, pp. 12.
27) Oct. 16, 1948.
28) Dempsey, *The New York Times*, May 11, 1958.
29) Theodor Geisel, quoted in *The Raleigh* (N.C.) *Times*, Jan. 6, 1951.
30) Geisel's Utah lecture notes, reprinted in Morgan and Morgan, pp. 123–124. Travers was, of course, the author of *Mary Poppins* and other books.
31) Geisel lecture notes, reprinted in Morgan and Morgan, pp. 124.
32) Louise Bonino to Theodor Geisel, Sept. 29, 1949, reprinted in Morgan and Morgan, pp. 124. Saxe Commins was an editor at Random House.

Four

1) Morgan and Morgan, pp. 128–129.
2) Sept. 1950, 26:354.
3) Nov. 12, 1950, pp. 8.
4) Nov. 11, 1950, pp. 33.
5) Nov. 19, 1950, pp. 42.
6) In Morgan and Morgan, pp. 134–135.
7) Donald Spoto. *Stanley Kramer, Film Maker*. (New York: G.P. Putnam's Sons, 1979), pp. 149.
8) Morgan and Morgan, pp. 135.
9) *Scrambled Eggs Super!*, no pagination.
10) March 29, 1953, pp. 14.
11) May 17, 1953, pp. 10.
12) Sept. 1953.
13) *Life*, March 29, 1954.
14) Morgan and Morgan, pp. 137.

15) The *Movies Unlimited* Catalogue, which lists "thousands and thousands" of films now available in VCR format, does not list *The 5,000 Fingers of Dr. T.*
16) E.J. Kahn Jr. interview with Phyllis Jackson, reprinted in Morgan and Morgan, pp. 140–141.
17) "All Time Best Selling Hardcover Children's Books," *Publishers Weekly* magazine, Feb. 5, 1996.
18) Morgan and Morgan, pp. 145.
19) *Horton Hears a Who!*, no pagination.
20) Geisel, quoted in Morgan and Morgan, notes for pp. 144.
21) May 24, 1954.
22) Morgan and Morgan, pp. 148.
23) Ibid., pp. 150.
24) Oct. 24, 1954, pp. 20.
25) Sept. 1, 1954. *Kirkus* is a publication for librarians which recommends books for library purchase.
26) Sept. 12, 1954, pp. 32.
27) In Morgan and Morgan, pp. 151.
28) *Colliers* magazine, Dec. 23, 1954, pp. 86.
29) *On Beyond Zebra!*, no pagination.
30) Oct. 15, 1955.
31) Nov. 13, 1955, pp. 3.
32) Nov. 13, 1955, pp. 45.
33) Morgan and Morgan, pp. 152.
34) *If I Ran the Circus*, no pagination.
35) Nov. 18, 1956, pt. 2, pp. 47.
36) Nov. 17, 1956.
37) Nov. 11, 1956, pp. 2.
38) Nov. 24, 1956.
39) Nov. 11, 1956, pp. 11.
40) John C. Fuller, "Trade Winds" column, *The Saturday Review of Literature*, Dec. 14, 1957.
41) Dr. Seuss, "How Orlo Got His Book," *The New York Times Book Review.* Nov. 15, 1957.
42) Theodor Geisel, quoted in Morgan and Morgan, pp. 154.

Five

1) Dr. Seuss, *The Cat in the Hat*, no pagination.
2) Karla Kuskin, "The Mouse in the Corner, the Fly on the Wall: What Very Young Eyes See in Picture Books," *The New York Times Book Review*, Nov. 14, 1993.
3) How can you determine whether you have a first edition of a book, or a reprint edition? The page behind the main title page should show copyright; and toward the bottom of the page, if there is a line of numbers, the lowest number indicates the reprint edition. In this case, the copy of *The Cat in the Hat* I have shows: 104 103 102 101 100 99. My copy is part of the 99th printing. What that printing is sold out and the book goes back to press—as it invariably will—the 99 is erased and then the 100 will be the reprint edition. This is Random House. Other firms have other methods of showing first editions. At Charles Scribners Sons, in the late 1930s and 1940s, first editions of Hemingway books and others were shown by an A on the copyright page. The A was then erased for a reprinting. The editions and reprintings, however, do not tell the reader anything about how many books constitute a second printing, or in the case of *The Cat in the Hat,* how many books were printed during the 99th reprinting. Nor do the reprint numbers necessarily indicate the rare book value of the copy.
4) March 17, 1957, pp. 40.
5) May 12, 1957, pp. 24.
6) May 12, 1957, pt. 2, pp. 7.
7) May 11, 1957.
8) April, 1957.
9) *How the Grinch Stole Christmas!*, Random House, 1957, no pagination.
10) Morgan and Morgan, pp. 58.
11) Ibid., pp. 160.
12) Nov. 16, 1957.

13) Nov. 10, 1957, pp. 20.
14) Oct. 6, 1957, pp. 40.
15) Nov. 17, 1957, pp. 30.
16) Sept. 15, 1957.
17) Morgan and Morgan, pp. 158.
18) Ibid., pp. 159.
19) Geisel, op. cit, in Morgan and Morgan, pp. 160.
20) Morgan and Morgan, pp. 165–166.
21) Nov. 1, 1958
22) Nov. 2, 1958, pt. 2, pp. 11.
23) Nov. 15, 1958.
24) Nov. 1958.
25) Nov. 2, 1958, pt. 2, pp. 8.
26) Cynthia Gorney, "Dr. Seuss at 75: Grinch, Cat in Hat Wocket and Generations of Kids in His Pocket," *The Washington Post*, May 21, 1979.
27) May 1, 1958.
28) August, 1958.
29) May 11, 1958.
30) Sept. 20, 1958.
31) *Happy Birthday to You!*, no pagination.
32) Dec. 1959. Ms. Jackson seems to have confused the Birthday Bird, which flew with the child and the Smorgasbord which carried the child as it loped along, a Seussian cross between a horse and (perhaps) a llama.
33) Dec. 1960.
34) Jan. 15, 1960.
35) *One Fish, Two Fish, Red Fish, Blue Fish*, pp. 38–39.
36) May 8, 1960, sec. 12, pp. 21.
37) May 7, 1960.
38) May 12, 1960, pp. 4B.
39) March 20, 1960, pp. 42.
40) Morgan and Morgan, pp. 167.
41) *Green Eggs and Ham*, pp. 9–16.
42) Jones, op cit, in Morgan and Morgan, pp. 170–171.

43) Morgan and Morgan, pp. 171.
44) Michael J., Bandler, "Seuss on the Loose," *Parents* magazine, Sept. 1987.
45) Sept. 15, 1960.
46) Book Review section, Nov. 13, 1960, sec. 12, pp. 16.
47) Nov. 19, 1960.
48) Nov. 12, 1960.
49) pp., 34.

Six

1) Cott, "The Good Dr. Seuss," from *Pipers at the Gates of Dawn*, pp. 28–29.
2) *The Sneetches and Other Stories*, no pagination.
3) Ibid.
4) Robert Bernstein, quoted in Morgan and Morgan, pp. 173–174.
5) Nov. 12, 1961, Sec. 2, pp. 12.
6) Oct. 28, 1961.
7) Morgan and Morgan, pp. 176.
8) *Dr. Seuss's Sleep Book*, no pagination.
9) Sept. 9, 1962, pp. 30.
10) Nov. 15, 1962, pp. 2B.
11) *Hop on Pop*, pp. 18–19, 23–24, 26–31.
12) *Dr. Seuss's ABC*, pp. 3–5, 6–8, 56–57, 61–63.
13) April 14, 1963, pp. 56.
14) June 5, 1963.
15) May 12, 1963, sec. 12, pp. 24.
16) Nov. 10, 1963, pt. 2, pp. 52.
17) Nov. 14, 1963, pp. 2B.
18) Morgan and Morgan, pp. 178.
19) *Hop on Pop*, pp. 62–63.
20) Morgan and Morgan, pp. 179.
21) *Fox in Sox*, pp. 47–48.
22) April 18, 1965, pp. 16.

23) May 6, 1965, pp. 2B.
24) We assume that Dr. Seuss knew he was using a variation on the French word for grapefruit: *pamplemousse*.
25) *I Had Trouble in Getting to Solla Sollew*, no pagination.
26) Morgan and Morgan, pp. 187.
27) Ibid., pp. 191.
28) Ibid., pp. 191.
29) The note became part of the Coroner's report on her death and was reprinted in Morgan and Morgan, pp. 195.
30) *The Foot Book*, no pagination.
31) Morgan and Morgan, pp. 200–201.
32) I was able to read a copy on loan from the Library of the University of South Carolina, Columbia. It is a very drab looking book—T.F.
33) *Esquire*, June 1974.
34) Geisel told the same story to his biographers, Morgan and Morgan (pp. 210) and to Chris Dummit of *The Dallas Morning News*, June 16, 1983.
35) *The Lorax*.
36) Nov. 11, 1971, pp. B4.
37) Nov. 15, 1971.
38) It is now in its forty-second printing.

Seven

1) *Marvin K. Mooney, Will You Please Go Now!* no pagination.
2) This episode appeared in "The Private World of Dr. Seuss" by Hillaird Harper, *The Los Angeles Times Magazine*, May 25, 1986.
3) *There's a Wocket in My Pocket!*, no pagination.
4) Morgan and Morgan, pp. 217–218.
5) His heart attack is described in Morgan and Morgan, pp. 245.
6) *The Butter Battle Book*, no pagination.
7) Ibid., no pagination.
8) Morgan and Morgan, pp. 250.

9) Ibid., pp. 252.
10) May, 1984.
11) March 2, 1984, pp. 2.
12) Morgan and Morgan, pp. 255.
13) Ibid., pp. 255.
14) Ibid., pp. 261.
15) *You're Only Young Once!*, no pagination.
16) Ibid., no pagination.
17) Morgan and Morgan, pp. 265.
18) Ibid., pp. 267–269.
19) *Oh! The Places You'll Go*, no pagination.
20) Morgan and Morgan, pp. 283.
21) "The Cabinet of Dr. Seuss."
22) Quoted in Morgan and Morgan, pp. 286.
23) Ibid., pp. 287.

Epilogue

1) Harper, "The Private World of Dr. Seuss," May 25, 1986.
2) *Time*, Oct. 7, 1991.

Index

About the Author

Thomas Fensch has published 18 books of nonfiction, including books about John Steinbeck, James Thurber, Oskar Schindler and Theodor Geisel. His biographies include: *Steinbeck And Covici; Conversations with John Steinbeck; Conversations with James Thurber; Oskar Schindler and His List* and *Of Sneetches and Whos and the Good Doctor Seuss.*

He holds a doctorate from Syracuse University and lives near Houston, Texas.

CPSIA information can be obtained
at www.ICGtesting.com
Printed in the USA
LVOW12*0144120218
566181LV00001B/9/P